The Mirrored Window

JUDITH LANGER

Senior Vice President
Roper/Langer Qualitative Division

ROPER STARCH WORLDWIDE

205 East 42nd Street
New York, NY 10017
tel: 212-599-0700
fax: 212-867-7008
www.roper.com
info@roper.com

JUDITH LANGER is Senior Vice President and Director, Roper/Langer Qualitative Division of Roper Starch Worldwide, Inc.

An expert on qualitative research and on lifestyle trends, Ms. Langer is often published in *Marketing News* and *Marketing Review.* A speaker at Advertising Research Foundation, American Association of Public Opinion Research and other professional conferences, she has been quoted on lifestyle and marketing trends by *CBS News, Cable News Network, Prime Time Live, The Wall Street Journal, The New York Times, USA Today, Adweek* and *Advertising Age.*

Ms. Langer has a background in public opinion and marketing research at Louis Harris, Roper Associates (predecessor of Roper Starch Worldwide), NBC, MPi Marketing Research and Lieberman Research West. She has conducted qualitative research since 1970, establishing her own company, Langer Associates, in 1979. She was the first president of the Qualitative Research Consultants Association and is a current member of its Board of Directors. She also serves on the the ARF Qualitative Council and has been a member of the American Marketing Association's Board of Directors. She has a certificate from the Creative Problem Solving Institute for its Springboard program.

In her few moments of spare time, she loves ballroom dancing, especially the waltz.

Ms. Langer received her B.A. in Government (Magna Cum Laude) from Smith College, and an M.A. in Government from Columbia University.

The Mirrored Window

The Mirrored Window

FOCUS GROUPS
from a Moderator's Point of View

Judith Langer

PMP

PARAMOUNT MARKET PUBLISHING, INC.

Paramount Market Publishing, Inc.
301 S. Geneva Street, Suite 109
Ithaca, NY 14850
www.paramountbooks.com
Telephone: 607-275-8100; 888-787-8100
Facsimile: 607-275-8101

Publisher: James Madden
Editorial Director: Doris Walsh

Library of Congress Catalog Number:
Cataloging in Publication Data available
ISBN 0-9671439-4-2

Book design and composition: Paperwork

CONTENTS

Acknowledgments

MANY THANKS: To Alison Stein Wellner for her hard work with me on the manuscript. To Naomi Brody, who has worked closely with me on many qualitative research studies and reviewed the book for me. To Cindi Gerber, Rose D'Amato, and Kathy Edwards for their help in keeping our office going and being so great to work with. To Jean Farinelli and Anita Hunter, who encouraged me to write the book. And, to Doris Walsh and Jim Madden of Paramount Market Publications who invited me to put down my thoughts on qualitative research. To my new colleagues at Roper Starch Worldwide for their conviction that a partnership of qualitative and quantitative research is valuable in tracking trends.

In particular, I'd like to thank several clients and research colleagues who gave me their time to be "respondents" for this book: Judi Alexander, Lynn Bircsak, Stephen Blacker, Jim Bryson, Echart Guthe, Terry Campion, Kathi Love, Steve Marlow, Scott McDonald, Kathleen O'Shaughnessy,

Wendy Robinson, Mike Schwartz, Andy Semons, Jim Spaeth, Elizabeth Tarpinian, Linda Thorp, Susan Walsh, and Barbara Zack.

Thanks to Ardith Talbot at McNeil Consumer Products and Terri Bunofsky at Playboy Enterprises for their permission to use case studies.

I'm very grateful for the interesting and gratifying life I've had as a qualitative researcher. For this, I thank the respondents I've spoken to and the many clients I've enjoyed working with over the years. Members of the Qualitative Research Consultants Association have always been generous, too, in sharing ideas and tips. The organization works hard to raise the level of quality in our field and it also helps make research constantly exciting even to seasoned "veterans" like me.

On the home front, love to Bernie Brachfeld, my dance partner in life, to my brother Bill Wollheim, and to Nudnik who gave support during the many hours I was stuck working on my computer.

INTRODUCTION

Qualitative research is becoming much more important. We need to better understand the right questions to ask in quantitative studies. **Live focus groups will always be necessary** because it's critical to really see how someone reacts in real time, instead of just reading their comments in a chat room.

—Stephen Blacker
Senior Vice President,
Market Research,
Condé Nast Publications

How it starts

THE PHONE RINGS. It's a woman I never met before. Her name is Ardith Talbot, and she's research director at McNeil Consumer Products. She tells me that someone else in her company has recommended me and that while they have other moderators they regularly work with, they are always looking for someone new. And she has a project in mind. The company is planning to introduce a new product, Motrin Migraine, and they are awaiting FDA approval. They have an "agency creative brief"— their ad agency has developed some ideas for an ad campaign, but they haven't tested their concepts yet. McNeil wants to figure out how to position the product, that is, how to differentiate it from others in the category. Competitors are already out there in the marketplace. The questions are: how does Motrin get an "ownable" positioning? How can they leverage the prescription background of Motrin? What advertising strategies will best communicate their message to consumers, create interest in the product, and best fit the brand?

We start to discuss who we'd want to talk to in the focus groups. Ardith tells me that she wants to include women who are self-diagnosed migraine sufferers, or women with severe headaches who believe they have migraines. When we get off the phone, she sends me a specific list of criteria, including demographic characteristics, for the type of people she'd like to see in the group, and she sends me the dates for the groups. There will be three daytime groups and two evening groups.

Facilities are like good hotels; they get booked quickly. That same day, my office put holds on focus group facilities in Philadelphia and Southern New Jersey, convenient to McNeil's offices. Later that same day, we decide on a facility near Philadelphia that we've used before and liked, and so we cancel our hold at the other facilities.

Our next step is to write the screener questionnaire that the facility will use to literally "screen" people for our focus groups. The screener is nine pages long and has sixteen questions. Of those, several are standard: a few demographic questions to make sure we have a mix of incomes, ages, and occupations; a "security" question to avoid having competitors in the groups; an "articulateness" question to make sure participants can express their feelings verbally. Five questions are specific to the person's physical condition as it relates to migraines, product usage, and attitudes about migraines and migraine products. We send it to Ardith for approval, and then we send it to the facility. The facility starts calling people in their database to see if they qualify for the group, inviting those who do to the group. This process takes approximately two weeks. In the meantime, the facility regularly sends us "breakdown sheets," which show us the names of the people who qualify. We are able to also see their answers to the key screener questions, which helps us know for sure whether we want them in the groups.

Meanwhile, we start working on the topic guide. I work closely with Ardith. During our discussions, we jump around, touching on all of the topics they need to cover, and I suggest different questions and techniques that I can use to get at that information during the group. I suggest that we start with general questions, asking about what a migraine feels like, and getting descriptions of the times that the people have experienced migraines. Then we plan to get into the way respondents treat their migraines. Next we'll talk about brands of medication. Then, because this is to help create an advertising campaign, I plan to ask the respondents to describe how they'd feel if their headaches were eliminated, whether in fantasy or real life. Then we have to ask about the advertising concepts, and I plan to have respondents write down their thoughts ahead of time so that the group won't bias them. Then we are to look at general "positioning" concepts, competitive brands and their ads, and other new marketing concepts. The topic guide is seven pages long. Whew! All this for two-hour groups! I am concerned about how I will ever hit on this many issues in such a short period.

Two weeks later, it is time for the focus groups. I arrive at the facility on the day of the groups about an hour ahead of time. I meet the client team. Ardith is there, as well as people from their advertising agency and others from McNeil. The first thing that we have to talk about is how to fit everything into the two-hour groups. We decide to have the respondents rank the advertising concepts quickly, and then focus in depth on the concepts that have the greatest interest. This will save time during the group. We also have to drop out quite a lot of material from the topic guide.

The respondents start arriving. We have to rescreen, which means we ask them the key product usage questions again, to make extra sure that they are indeed qualified, and to check the accuracy of our information. Sure enough, some information has to be updated and some respondents are dropped.

Finally, the clients are in the back room. I'm sitting up front with the respondents, and I take a deep breath and get started. The groups go well, the respondents open up and frankly discuss their migraines, giving vivid descriptions of the situations and their feelings. One woman actually gets a migraine during the group—first-hand observation for the clients in the back room. (She decides to go home.) From time to time, I go into the back room to see if the clients have any other questions. By the end of two groups, I know the project so well that I am able to boil the topic guide down into one page of handwritten notes. All I need are reminders of key topics and issues to probe. After four of the five groups are done, the clients and I get together for a debrief to discuss what we have learned so far, and anything that we want to do differently in the final group. I write a report within the next few weeks, and McNeil is able to use the findings to move ahead with their advertising campaign.

This is a typical focus group project, if any focus group project can be considered typical. In the pages that follow, you'll learn more about each step of the process, from creating a screener to analyzing results.

_____ *A personal note*

I started doing qualitative research in the early 1970s. I had been doing quantitative research and never really liked it. I had been drawn to research because I wanted to understand people better, but I didn't feel I was learning anything about them by devising and later analyzing closed-end questions. When I tried to visualize the respondents, the different user groups, I didn't have any sense of them. Where the data were inconsistent, I couldn't make sense of the contradictions.

When I started doing focus groups and depth interviews I found the experience fascinating, exciting, and fulfilling, given my interest in human motivation and behavior. I was working for the now defunct MPi (with Emanuel Demby and Lou Cohen). The company involved all its analysts in focus groups, which were routinely conducted as the first step in any major study. Later MPi reorganized and I became the qualitative specialist.

At the time, another researcher asked me if I was worried

about burnout doing groups and in-depth interviews. Decades later the answer is still, "No." I believe I would have burned out long ago if I had been pinned down to a desk writing and analyzing questionnaires. If you love qualitative research—and you should do it only if you love it—you don't burn out, except for short periods of time. Veteran qualitative researchers I've met through the Qualitative Research Consultants Association (QRCA) also express excitement about their work, even after years of experience.

Qualitative research isn't just a job, it's a lifestyle

While I continue to be enthusiastic, I realize I was naïve about the demands of qualitative research. I enjoyed talking with people, puzzling out what it all means. But I didn't realize that qualitative research isn't just a job, it's a lifestyle. The long hours and constant travel make it a highly demanding occupation that affects your personal life. You have to feel sure it's worth the trade-offs.

This book is a compilation of what I've learned throughout the years. My hope is that through reading it, you will become savvy where I was once naïve.

Sure, there are moments when interviewing loses its pleasure and even its interest. These are the moments of burnout, fortunately infrequent and short-lived. They can happen when I'm doing 20 depth interviews or 12 focus groups in a row on the same subject; when the dynamics of an entire group don't work; and during the "combat groups" when everyone hates the client's product, when everyone talks at once or when respondents are reluctant to talk, or when groups are intensely boring.

However, the good part of qualitative research is that it's fun—most of the time. The variety of the projects and the people we meet make it different, surprising, and special.

Within two days, clients called about possible projects on a new kind of toilet seat and precious jewelry. In one week, I interviewed women about an inexpensive powdered beverage and women with $200,000-plus incomes who had gone to luxury spas. In each case, we have to adapt our manner, wardrobe, and vocabulary to the people we are interviewing. Having spent most of my life in Manhattan, I feel fortunate to be able to meet so many people different from myself. Usually I find I like them and, despite different backgrounds, share feelings in common.

The process itself remains fascinating. No matter how long you've done qualitative research, you can still develop your skills further and learn new techniques for getting at the truth.

I have found that beyond the confines of the commissioned studies, there is so much to discover about consumers — the way they live, how they view their lives, what they believe, what they want for themselves, what they think of what's going on in the world. Mundane subjects often reveal a great deal about how people live their lives. Studying laundry products over a period of years, we find that not only has the market changed, but family life and lifestyles have also changed. So beyond discussing how to design and execute a qualitative research project, I will also share with you some of my observations about consumers.

All these years of talking with people have affected me as a person. I've learned a lot about my own motivations and reactions, since the first respondent on any study is yourself. During the interviews, I have been struck by the ways I'm either the same or different from the respondents. It's often clear in our research how much we all limit

No matter how long you've done qualitative research, you can still develop your skills further and learn new techniques for getting at the truth

ourselves by mental pigeonholes of what we should and shouldn't do. I've learned to think through what I really feel and want, not just what society has told me.

Warning: Qualitative research is compelling. My retirement plan is to interview until I drop. I hope that this book will convey the excitement and enchantment that occur when you step inside the room with the mirrored window.

Part 1
What, When, and How

Part1
What, When, and How

CHAPTER 1

When to Do Qualitative Research

> **The purpose of focus groups is different from quantitative research.** In focus groups, you want to show the product and get reactions, or have a theory and have it discussed, or have concepts fleshed out for the quantitative research in the customer's own words.
>
> —*Susan Walsh*
> The Hearst Corporation

Let's get started

WHO ARE OUR CUSTOMERS? What kinds of people are they? How do they talk? How do they think? How do they see themselves? How do they live? How do they feel about our product? How should we talk to them? What do they want and need? What do they think of us? Finding the answers to questions like these is the primary reason why focus groups and in-depth interviews are used.

When companies start to ask these questions, they have varying degrees of knowledge. In some cases, there is a total information vacuum, and qualitative research is the first step in learning about the customers. In other cases, they already have a demographic profile of their customers, for instance, information about age, income, geographic area, occupation, and children in the home. This information is both crucial and incomplete — it's not alive or dynamic. What clients are missing is their customers' mindsets, what they feel, what motivates them, how they see themselves. The company may not even know why its customers buy the product or service, or why non-customers are avoiding it. Without answers, client companies don't know how to communicate with their markets or how to design products for them.

This gut-level grasp can give clients a sense of what is unique about their customers

The immediacy of the qualitative research experience provides clients with a gut-level grasp of their customers. I'm talking about deep, broad-ranging, experiential, intuitive insights that go beyond a list of their demographics, attitudes, and behavior. This gut-level grasp can give clients a sense of what is unique about their customers — the self-perceptions, the drives, and the needs that affect everything they do. It is a basic, comprehensive view that allows the client to enter into the customers' experiences and world in a way that numbers alone would never reveal.

For example, small-business owners have very different attitudes than Fortune 1000 corporate managers do about the separation between work and business. To small-business owners, their businesses are the same as their "real" or personal life. Addressing the two groups in the same way can mean failing to communicate, or worse, the messages can backfire.

Definition of terms

Client: The entity paying for the research.

Respondents: People who are interviewed during the qualitative research process.

Moderator: Many qualitative researchers don't like the term "moderator" since it focuses just on the interviewing. We handle much more than this. We're really consultants, recommending research designs, developing ideas, and suggesting implications. Some in the field prefer the term Qualitative Research Consultant (QR or QRC). The terms "moderator" and "QRC" are not synonymous because there are qualitative researchers who do not conduct interviews. While I agree about our broader role, I'm comfortable with "moderator" in this book as a good shorthand term.

For clients and for researchers, witnessing real people talking about their lives in real time packs an emotional wallop. We once held a focus group on money management and financial services with men and women over age 55. We had a lively, spirited, intelligent discussion among people who were involved and highly knowledgeable about their money. Observing from behind the one-way mirror was a small group of clients, ranging in age from late 20s to early 30s. "I can't believe the older people were so sharp," one client remarked in surprise at the end of the evening. This group unsettled the young clients' picture of "senior citizens" as rigid, old-fashioned, slow-witted and unsophisticated.

Why was a focus group able to drive this point home when the mass media, not to mention quantitative surveys, did not? My hypothesis is that information in the form of words and numbers is received on an intellectualized level. Seeing and hearing consumers only a few feet away has an effect that no set of statistics or written reports alone can have. It makes the abstract real because it is human and individual. Qualitative research offers not just an intellectual comprehension of consumers, but a vivid, visceral recognition that affects on a very deep level how companies see, feel about, and deal with their customers from then on.

To use qualitative research to its full potential, it is essential to recognize that words are just a starting place. Pay attention to the intensity in respondents' voices, their body language and their self-presentation, not just their words. Are they excited and involved, or are they angry, upset? Their responses can tell you a lot about your chances of persuading them. If their resistance seems strong and deep, it's a lot harder to capture their attention than if they

Qualitative research offers a vivid, visceral recognition that affects on a very deep level how companies see, feel about, and deal with their customers from then on

appear receptive, changing their minds when they hear new facts.

Debit cards to deodorant

A few years ago, we did several studies with consumers to explore the concept of debit cards. The user presents the card rather than cash, like a credit card, but the money immediately comes straight out of a checking account. The body language and statements of people in the group were very negative. It wasn't just that they said they disliked the idea. They pulled back from the table, shook their heads, pursed their lips tightly and, with evident vehemence, declared, "I would never let anyone get into my checking account." The mistrust — the sense of invaded privacy — suggested that resistance to this idea ran deep and that marketers would have to work hard to change consumer attitudes. In fact, it did take quite a while before these cards caught on.

The way people dress can also offer an important message about who they are and how they see themselves. In a study of female deodorant users, we conducted separate focus groups with users of a brand positioned specifically for young women, and users of other brands (most of them advertised to both sexes). Simply looking at the respondents showed how dramatically different the segments' self-images were. The users of the female-oriented brand wore clothing that was distinctly, even stereotypically, feminine — either innocent (pink and white, ruffles) or sexy (lots of jewelry and makeup, low necklines, Playboy T-shirts). Non-users of the female-oriented brand generally wore sporty and more tailored outfits. These divergent styles suggested that very different advertising approaches would be needed for each group—and, within the "feminine" segment, between the "girly-girl" and the "sexy" segments.

_____ ***Seeing inside the customers***

These observations often cannot easily be formalized and packaged into quantitative studies. Qualitative research allows us to see in consumers what they themselves may not be aware of and, therefore, what they cannot report in straightforward questioning. In addition, what is important and relevant in one category (how people dress or their energy level, for instance) may be meaningless in another. A standard set of psychographic variables would be simplistic and inadequate. Instead, we have to be open and receptive while observing respondents: What stands out about these people? What is the dominant feeling and impression they leave behind?

_____ ***To believe or not?***

The powerful impact of qualitative research is, of course, exactly what makes many researchers and marketers wary of the technique. The danger is that marketing personnel observing a session will listen selectively to one individual, then rush off and make major decisions based on this person's comments. Even after large-scale quantitative studies have been conducted, some people will believe isolated examples of what they saw in the groups ("Remember the woman in yellow in Columbus?") rather than the statistical research. This is especially true when the qualitative

Qualitative research allows us to see in consumers what they themselves may not be aware of

research seems to back someone's pet project. Some companies, in fact, go so far as to ban all qualitative research or all focus groups because of this danger.

The danger is real. The problem, however, is not with the qualitative research *per se*. It is with the actions of people who are not researchers and who do not understand the caveats we issue about sampling and question methods.

The answer is to consider what comes out of qualitative research as hypothesis, not absolute fact. The new picture of the consumer is a possibility to consider and to explore further through quantitative studies with larger samples and structured questionnaires.

There's also an opposite danger: Sometimes managers will not believe what they see in a focus group. Several years ago, we conducted a study on designer jeans. The fashion phenomenon had already passed its peak; the market had, so to speak, bottomed out. Respondents were all designer jeans purchasers, but they did not all match the client's expectation of highly fashion-conscious, trendy, skinny women. The client wanted to change the respondent specifications, requiring that all the women wear sizes six to ten only, and that they all read fashion magazines. If we had followed their suggestion (we talked them out of it), we would have been looking only at a select segment of jeans buyers.

Sometimes managers will not believe what they see in a focus group

Why did the clients reject what they saw? They wanted to believe they had glamorous, exciting customers who mirrored the disco lifestyle of their advertising. In addition, I think, they resisted the message that designer jeans were no longer a fashion-leader item, that they were a mass-market item accepted by the fashion followers.

Sometimes clients reject what they see because the customer is more sophisticated than they expected. For Zayre, a now defunct discount department store chain, we screened for women who shopped regularly at that type of store during a major economic recession. Expecting to observe a group of women who had low incomes and little education, this client was upset because some of the shoppers were too upscale and sophisticated. They shopped often at discount stores to find "brand names for less." What we witnessed was middle-class customers adapting themselves to a bad economy and reduced financial power, using their consumer savvy to get more for their money. They were shopping in stores they had looked down on not too long before.

Qualitative research can be an early barometer

The qualitative research was an early barometer of the economy's impact on store loyalties, the start of a new trend. Competitive stores like Wal-Mart succeeded because they offered shoppers a pleasant yet not fancy store environment, a place they enjoyed going for bargains, rather than one they tolerated with frustration for the sake of low prices. Conversely, upscale retailers are often upset when respondents in focus groups are not elegantly dressed (even in this informal era). Their perceptions of their customers tend to be based on what their very best, big-spending customers are like, not the mainstream shopper.

The "this-isn't-my-customer" response is more common with qualitative research. It is easier to blame the recruiting and the moderator. In a quantitative study, clients rarely see the respondents in person, so there are no images to clash with their preconceptions. The statistics in a study seem impersonal, detached from the researcher reporting them—and harder to attack.

New product development _____

There is another area where qualitative research is used with a great degree of success: development of new products. It is often in a focus group that new ideas are brought to consumers for feedback for the first time.

Qualitative research techniques could be brought even earlier into the new product development cycle. Thousands of dollars are often spent on research and development, just to find that consumers aren't having any, thank you. Bringing in consumers at the beginning of the process means that they can generate ideas, not just evaluate them. Because our questions are open-ended, stimulating consumers to answer in their own words, the process is designed to encourage serendipity. A comment by just one respondent can spark a money-making idea.

Because our questions are open-ended, the process is designed to encourage serendipity

It's important to note that ideas for new products rarely come directly from consumers' suggestions, but their comments and ideas often provide the spark that gets everyone's creative juices flowing. You do have to pay attention, because it happens when you least expect it. For example, we did groups for the United States Holocaust Memorial Museum in Washington, D.C. Museum members were shown five ideas for an annual calendar used as a fundraiser. They liked one best, but said it was too good an idea to be only a calendar that would be thrown away when the year was over. Instead, they suggested it should be made into a book that would be kept forever as part of a person's home and given to others as a meaningful gift. As a result, the Museum went with the second best idea for the calendar and published the preferred idea as a book, and it was a big success.

Examples of appropriate issues for qualitative research:

- We're not sure who our market is. Who uses our product and why?

- We don't know how to speak to our market. What language and images can we use?

- We don't know what consumers think of our new product idea. What are the selling points? How can it be improved?

- We don't know why they've stopped buying our product. We want to uncover the real reasons beyond the pat answers of time and price.

- We know we need to do something to boost sales, and we don't know what it is.

- We need to create new products, but we don't know what they should be.

- We need new ideas for an ad campaign.

- We need to understand what our advertising communicates.

- We want to know if a new program we are developing appeals to our users and how we can improve it.

- We need new ideas for packaging. We want to know if consumers can use our packaging.

- We want to know what our brand image is vs. our competitors'.

- How do we market our audience to our advertisers? (for magazines and newspapers)

- What are our customers' lifestyles? Who are they and what do they care about?

Examples of issues *not* appropriate for qualitative research:

- We need to make a multimillion-dollar decision based only on this research.

- We want a definitive answer on the top-three reasons why people buy our product.

- We need to find out the demographics of our customers.

- We need to know the size of different market segments.

CHAPTER 2

High Tech Comes to High Touch

> Right now, online qualitative research is in a very rudimentary stage. The Internet has a lot of problems because you lose so much of the face-to-face richness and interaction—you don't have body language, voice inflection, and non-verbal cues. What the Internet is good for today is cognitive decision-making research. But that will begin to change. **Online research is growing at about 100 to 150 percent a year.**
>
> *—Jim Bryson, President*
> Qualitative Research Consultants Association, and President of Research Concepts and 20/20 Research and QualTalk.com

Focus groups in an era of change

FOCUS GROUPS ARE HARDLY NEW. They have been around in market research since the 1940s. When I started in the early 1970s, they were already a very well-established technique, though constantly belittled for being "unscientific." At that point, few people outside market- and public-opinion research had any idea what a focus group was. ("What *is* it you do?" my mother asked after I had been a moderator for ten years.)

Since then, the use of focus groups has grown enormously. There are still some detractors in the marketing and advertising community, of course, but focus groups are a standard part of most research programs. In the 1990s, focus groups also broke into public consciousness. Television shows like *Thirtysomething, Murphy Brown, The West Wing* and *Frasier* have all featured focus groups. A common scenario is to show newscasters or advertising agency creatives going crazy hearing schlubby, uninformed respondents saying terrible things about them. Bill Clinton used the technique extensively in both of his presidential campaigns, along with surveys; so did the candidates in 2000.

Public interest in focus groups is part of a growing fascination with media and marketing. People want to know how things are done; they want to be in on the game, to know how companies or politicians are selling to them. It's common for ordinary consumers to use marketing language today. In some recent focus groups, I asked teenagers for their reactions to a publication. First they wanted to know "Who's the target audience?" That's marketing terminology few people, especially young ones, would have used a few years ago.

People want to know how things are done; they want to be in on the game, to know how companies or politicians are selling to them

On the one side, a number of qualitative researchers are pleased that, at last, people have heard of our occupation. This not only helps attract business but it may increase willingness to participate in focus groups rather than be suspicious that the research is a ruse for selling.

On the other side, as awareness of focus groups has grown, so have media scrutiny, skepticism and sometimes downright hostility. *The New York Times* columnist Frank Rich wrote in 2000, "Focus groups have a clout unmatched by labor unions or the religious right." Articles talk with disdain about the fact that companies "focus grouped" an idea. (Ugh — "focus group" as a verb.) The implication is that the politician or company is pandering — that the product, the movie, the message is decided based on what a handful of people in some focus groups say. The issue, of course, is not so simple. It's obvious that politicians want to win elections, companies want to sell their products and services. Those have always been the goals.

Focus groups are one more form of "intelligence" about voters, the audience, consumers. They enable researchers and clients to understand the mindset of their target group on a deeper level than quantitative surveys (which are also used). Good qualitative research always keeps in mind that our "hypotheses" are just that; no matter how common sense they appear to be, we can't be sure they're right. We analyze what we hear with sophisticated judgment, rather than taking focus group comments at face value. And good researchers suggest new ideas and modifications to benefit the client, while bearing in mind that the changes need to respect the integrity of the "product." You can't just slap a happy ending on a movie, tell a politician to be something she isn't and doesn't want to be, advise a newspaper to abandon its journalistic standards.

This is a particularly interesting time for focus groups, too, because qualitative research is undergoing dramatic changes. Focus groups with clients watching from behind the mirrored window remain the central qualitative research technique and, I believe, will continue to be. However, two apparently opposite trends are taking place simultaneously, both at the high tech and the high touch ends of the spectrum.

High Tech: the Internet comes to focus groups

The most "touchy-feely" type of research is being affected by technology, in the way qualitative research is con-

The Internet has become a staple of the American way of life, used by many "ordinary" people of all ages and both genders

ducted, the way clients participate and, to a lesser extent, in the analysis. The biggest wave has been in Internet research.

In the last five years, there has been a surge of interest in researching the online population. A number of the big companies in quantitative research have started online panels of consumers that they survey. There have been debates about whether those panels are representative of the U.S. population, although the debate has started to fade as the Internet has become more mainstream.

Attitudes toward the Internet have changed dramatically among consumers, business people, and the marketing and market research communities. Until only recently, the Internet was a medium for "techies," a small minority of the public who were mostly young men. Today, the Internet has become a staple of the American way of life, used by many "ordinary" people of all ages and both genders.

"Complementarity" is a major trend in our society today as the Internet and the physical world increasingly work together or supplement one another. [See chapter 10.] Almost every week, it seems, I receive a brochure about a conference on Internet research. Predictions that online survey and qualitative research will replace in-person focus groups have become common. The language used to talk about online research often reveals a bias in its favor: in-person focus groups are referred to as "traditional" (i.e., old-fashioned) or "offline" (i.e., not online — defined by what they aren't).

In reality, however, in-person focus groups continue to flourish. It is telling that some of the biggest Internet companies choose to do in-person groups to understand their

It's difficult to develop an objective view of the strengths and weaknesses of online research at this early stage

Online Focus Groups

ADVANTAGES

▶ *Quick recruiting*

▶ *Broader groups are affordable*

▶ *Locate low-incidence respondents*

▶ *Bring together people from different locations who share a common world*

▶ *Less group bias*

▶ *Lower cost*

▶ *Transcripts available immediately*

users. One Web site company admitted during a conference Q&A that, although it is "heresy," she found the "offline" focus groups more valuable than the online ones they had held. Why would such companies, the most high tech of all, want to sit behind a mirror at a facility rather than at their computers in the office or, better yet, at home? The answer is simple. In-person focus groups make it possible for clients to see their users, to hear them, to find out how truly interested they are (or aren't) in the Web site vs. competitors. A recent study we conducted, for instance, helped the client figure out why some consumers became loyal and repeat visitors, while others dropped out after a few visits. To the client's surprise, behavior did not necessarily relate to the user's level of Internet sophistication. Instead, it related to their feelings about the site's content. This insight might not have been possible in an online study.

It's difficult to develop an objective view of the strengths and weaknesses of online research at this early stage. Online focus groups are new and, therefore, exciting, to a number of qualitative researchers and clients. Let's admit that the novelty in itself has appeal. The view that in-person focus groups are "traditional" makes them seem more out of date.

Based on our own experience in moderating and reviewing online qualitative research, I believe that this will be one more method, not the sole one, in the future. Online groups can offer some quick answers but for issues which require greater depth, for the full impact of the qualitative experience, I think clients will still want to see and hear people firsthand.

Advantages of online focus groups

Speed of recruiting is usually just a few days versus the typical two weeks for in-person groups.

Groups can include geographically dispersed respondents, without travel costs or time. Many clients and moderators would prefer staying home to hitting the road.

Low-incidence respondents can be found — people who may represent a small percentage of the total population. The extent to which an online research company can do this, however, depends on its particular panel; don't automatically assume it's possible to locate that haystack needle.

People from different locations who share a common world can be brought together. In the case of employee research, for instance, people around the country or the world can share their thoughts with anonymity. Or high-level executives can exchange views with their peers without leaving their offices.

Less group bias. This is a main claim for online focus groups, one that needs to be tested further. Because respondents submit their answers around the same time and prior to seeing what others wrote, they may be more likely to be independent. For better or worse, respondents also seem not to notice what other people are saying much of the time. This does not mean that the group effect is totally eliminated, of course. In some sessions, there still can be a big positive or negative wave of reaction.

Costs are lower than face-to-face groups in most instances. One factor is the lack of travel and entertainment; another is that the incentive fees paid to respondents are usually lower.

Online Focus Groups

DISADVANTAGES

▶ *Less screening security*
▶ *Less chance to probe*
▶ *Short responses are less rich*
▶ *Respondents don't interact*
▶ *More honest, or just more rude?*
▶ *Sense of individual is less clear*
▶ *Body language, vocal inflections are lost*
▶ *Disruptive technical problems*

Transcripts can be produced in much less time, often overnight. This process takes a little longer if they are edited so that the responses are put in the right sequence.

Disadvantages and issues of online focus groups

A bulletin board can feel like simultaneous depth interviews rather than a true focus group

Are respondents actually who they say they are? This is one of the most important obstacles to greater use of online research. Some recruiting companies make a point of phoning respondents to verify they at least sound like the gender they claim to be. How can we be sure that someone else hasn't substituted for a respondent halfway through the group? Certainly, there are issues of truthfulness associated with in-person research, too. However, in an in-person focus group we usually can tell (with some rare exceptions!) a respondent's gender, general age group, ethnic group. We also know that it's the same person throughout the two hours.

Online focus group sessions are shorter, usually 90 minutes, so there is less opportunity for discussion and probing.

Responses tend to be short, less rich than in-person ones. It's easier to talk than to type.

Interaction is limited. While the online medium is called "interactive," how much moderator-respondent and respondent-respondent interaction really takes place if respondents are busy typing? This is the flip side of less group bias. Based on my experience so far, respondents do not read one another's answers much of the time.

Understanding individuals. It is difficult for the moderator and observers to get as clear a sense of individual respondents as they can in an in-person group.

Body language and vocal inflection are missing. These important cues to emotions are not yet possible to observe in online research, and without them, marketers will not know how to communicate with different segments. Unfortunately, emoticons (smiling faces, winks, etc.) are not an adequate substitute.

Technical problems can arise that interrupt the focus group, knocking respondents or the moderator offline.

Some researchers believe that online research allows respondents to answer more honestly. Because respondents don't see one another, they are freer to express their thoughts and reveal personal information. On the other side, the in-person environment can at times make people more comfortable about sharing.

Several video-conferencing companies now compete with one another, each with a line-up of field services around the country

Online Bulletin Boards

The online bulletin board offers another Internet alternative which I find very promising. While the online focus group is done in real time, with everyone answering simultaneously, the bulletin board is stretched over several days or weeks. Respondents are asked to check in periodically to see the new questions, at their convenience. They have the chance to reflect on their answers, with less pressure to type quickly. As a result, their answers tend to be longer, more thoughtful. The technique makes it possible to follow people's decision-making over a period of time, to interview them immediately after a particular experience while it is still fresh in their minds. Again, it is possible to bring together people from different geographic areas, which can enrich some studies. A bulletin board can feel like simultaneous depth interviews rather than a true focus group. However, it can still be difficult to stimulate real interaction among respondents.

Other technology-based tools

The Internet isn't the only technological change in the focus-group world.

VIDEO CONFERENCING involves a large, mysterious-looking box with a video camera in the focus group room at connected facilities that transmits live pictures to clients sitting together in a room. Several client companies have set up special connections so they can observe from their offices — a fairly expensive procedure. The moderator still needs to travel (I was told recently that one study was done with the moderator in a different city from the respondents, however); and, in most cases, at least one client representative goes along. During the session, clients can communicate by phone, asking more questions and, at the end of the interviewing day, there is a debriefing with the moderator. Without this, a videotape could just be sent back to the client.

The advantages are obvious: less time out of the office for highly stressed executives and much lower travel expenses. Several video-conferencing companies now compete with one another, each with a line-up of field services around the country.

We have had relatively little call for this service, perhaps because we're based in New York. By the time a two-hour focus group in Chicago that starts at 8:00 p.m. is over, it's 11:00 p.m. on the East Coast. If the group is

WHAT
TECHNOLOGY
CAN DO
FOR YOU

▶ *Video Conferencing*

▶ *Internet Viewing*

▶ *Digital Recording*

▶ *Computer-assisted Analysis*

in Los Angeles, it's 1:00 a.m. the next day before New York clients would see the end of it.

Sometimes clients have inquired about video conferencing and then changed their minds because of the expense of the special connections, the late hours, or because they still want to be there in the back room, which feels more immediate. There are difficulties in setting up multi-market studies, too, if we want to use facilities without the hook-up or we're in areas that do not have it available. When an editor in New York could not attend focus groups in Atlanta because of severe back pain, we suggested the idea of video conferencing, but she chose instead to postpone until she could go in person for the firsthand experience.

Software packages can be helpful in qualitative analysis without doing the actual analysis

INTERNET VIEWING on a personal computer is another option for remote observation. "You can watch from anywhere you have Internet access, be it an office, a hotel room, or your home," and "chat with your colleagues who are also watching," one company's ad states. The "client lounge" on the screen shows the focus group room on one side and the clients' conversation on the other. The video made of the group can later be accessed on CD, giving users the flexibility of being able to jump to specific portions of the video. Personal-computer viewing is also less expensive than video conferencing.

Current applications of Internet viewing raise two immediate concerns. First, the picture of the focus group is quite small, which makes it difficult to see respondents' faces and the subtlety of their expressions. Clients may become more absorbed in their own conversations, losing sight, literally, of the session. But, given that Internet observation is a great savings in time and costs for clients, it would not be surprising to find that interest in this technology will grow.

DIGITAL RECORDING, both audio and video, is a new and growing practice. A "real-time audio organizer" makes it possible for the moderator and/or observer to mark good verbatim text in the interview, then go back and just listen to these excerpts. Good quotes can be marked by up to three clients in the back room (this helps to offset the bias of one client picking comments), indicating where each falls in the topic guide. Afterward, verbatims from all of the sessions can be combined and edited far more easily than regular audiotape. The quotes can be delivered on audiotape or CD-ROM or even integrated into an electronic version of the report. Some moderators clip quotes so they can review focus group highlights for their report; we are concerned that this may leave out important points. Our preference is to use the technology to bring the project to life, especially for people who did not attend the sessions. For our telephone depth interviews, we have added digital quotes or "sound bites" with our written reports so clients can literally listen to "the voice of the consumers," and hear how excited or angry they are. The purpose is to simplify the hours-long process of tape editing.

COMPUTER-ASSISTED ANALYSIS. Software packages for qualitative research analysis are still being used mainly by academics, in large part because they are quite time-consuming. On the simplest level, the software can count up the number of times certain words are said, a quantitative measure. The problem, of course, is that the same words might be said by the same repetitive respondent or by respondents repeating what the first one said.

Software packages can be helpful in qualitative analysis without doing the actual analysis. They can, for instance, sort out responses in individual interviews or focus groups by topic. Particularly in larger qualitative projects that can seem overwhelming (we once did a study with 287 half-hour depth interviews by phone, huge by qualitative standards), these programs can divide responses by question and respondent subgroup (gender, age, etc.). The ability to automatically organize the material is an enormous help.

High touch

Ethnographic or observational research has, at the same time, also become "hot" in qualitative research. These are interviews in what might be called people's natural habitats, an anthropological approach. People are interviewed and observed in their homes, their offices, in stores as they shop, in places they congregate with others (bars, restaurants, etc.). The researcher takes notes and often pictures, sometimes with a client in tow. This approach has several possible benefits: learning about what people *really* do, rather than rely on their self-reports (they claim to be health-conscious but their kitchen is filled with high fat foods); putting them more at ease than they might be in a conference room; refreshing their minds about the real-life experience instead of reconstructing it from memory.

On the other side, there are issues about the extent to which people posture for the camera and observers, and the fact that the technique can be very expensive and time-consuming.

Totally apart from its trendiness, my guess is that ethnographic research will continue to grow in popularity as we look for ways of understanding people's behavior. This technique will probably complement focus groups, which provide more of an opportunity to probe attitudes and emotions, to provoke good respondent interaction and — again — to bring clients and researchers together for that firsthand experience of observing the conversation.

The future of qualitative research will, I believe, include more high-tech applications. The technologies that will succeed will aid qualitative research's high touch value — not undermine it.

CHAPTER 3

Gearing Up for Groups

> Quantitative research is like a machine; who's at the helm doesn't matter. **Qualitative research is all about the moderator.**
> —*Jim Spaeth*, President and CEO
> The Advertising Research Foundation

_____ STEP 1: *To focus group or not to focus group?*

"WE WANT TO DO FOCUS GROUPS." Even though I make my living by doing qualitative research, these words don't necessarily excite me. Sometimes clients ask for focus groups without understanding whether this kind of research is appropriate to their objectives. Now that focus groups are better known—people have at least heard the term—it is not unusual for someone at a client company to say, "We need focus groups" when they want information about their market. Vague and unrealistic objectives need to be dealt with at the outset to determine if the research should even be attempted. Focus groups are just one research tool. There are other qualitative research approaches that may be better for a particular project. Sometimes quantitative research is the answer. Other times there may be no need for research at all.

A good rule of thumb:

■ Do qualitative research to get new ideas, to uncover mindsets and perceptions, feelings and emotions.

■ If the goal of research is to get numbers (how many) or just to find out behavior (what people do) without the "whys," do quantitative research instead.

A common mistake on the part of clients is to tell the moderator what questions to ask without giving background on the study as a whole. "We want to know how media buyers view our magazine." Why? "Because we have a problem in attracting advertising since agencies put us in a small niche." Now that's an issue we can study. The situation is like a patient coming to a doctor and saying, "Give me a pill." For what problem? Clients sometimes seem annoyed going through this process, but without a full explanation and background, moderators can't do a good job.

For focus groups to work well, there needs to be a clearly defined problem for the research to study.

Use **Qualitative Research** if you want:

■ Feelings, emotional side (the "touchy-feely"part qualitative research is famous for)

■ Motivations, underlying reasons

■ Mindsets, perceptions

■ New observations on behavior (qualitative research uncovers behavior as well as feelings)

■ Respondent interaction, such as word-of-mouth dynamics

■ Consumer language

■ Consumers to come to "life" for client

■ Video for research and/or promotional purposes

Use **Quantitative Research** if you want:

- Hard-core facts and numbers
- Behavior facts — usage, frequency, amount bought/used, etc
- Brand and advertising tracking of changes in awareness over time
- Market penetration (what percentage of households own a product)
- Information for pricing decisions
- Data to support multimillion-dollar decisions

All of these are perfectly acceptable objectives for qualitative research. They'll all require probing and follow up to make sure that the client and I understand each other. But if I hear these general categories, I know that qualitative research is appropriate. Focus groups won't give the clients absolute answers but they should provide good insights.

_____ STEP 2: *Choose the right qualitative researcher*

One of the first steps for a client in any project, qualitative or quantitative, is to choose the research company. In qualitative research, the choice of the moderator is especially critical, and it can get tricky. The moderator really runs the whole project, typically handling all of the interviewing in an intentionally open-ended and serendipitous process. If the moderator lacks rapport with the respondents, fails to understand what the project is really about, doesn't grasp the product, or doesn't know when and how to follow up interesting answers, the project will fail. In most cases, too, the moderator oversees the fieldwork — selecting the field service for its physical facility, making sure that the right respondents are screened for the focus groups. Even with the best moderator, if the respondents are wrong for the project, the research can also be worthless. Qualitative researchers also play a role from the very beginning in discussing issues like the research design, who the respondents should be, markets for the study and, of course, the interview guide. And the qualitative researcher's judgment at the end in analyzing what respondents have said is especially critical since, unlike quantitative research that has specific numbers (x% said this or that), interpretation is more complex. Qualitative researchers, then, usually are far more than just the "moderator" who asks respondents questions. They have to be good researchers and good project managers.

Qualitative

researchers

have to be good

researchers and

good project

managers

For clients choosing a new moderator, it is difficult to know who will do a good job. Word-of-mouth recommendations are heavily relied on. It's a lot like finding any other new professional service provider. For some clients, the reference is enough, but it's usually a good idea to talk with or meet the moderator. Why can't a moderator just show a prospective client tapes of focus groups and reports that he or she has done for prior clients? In fact, if a moderator does this, clients should worry about the confidentiality of their information. The exceptions are non-proprietary work done years ago for a client in a completely different field, or a self-funded project. Clients often have to evaluate the moderator based on an interview. Even this may not give the client a good sense of what the moderator is like in the focus groups. (I'm opinionated in meetings but remain neutral in the groups, for instance.)

Of course, there are clients who choose a moderator based on price. Important as budget realities are, price should not be the only factor to consider. If that sounds like pure self-interest on my part, I follow this principle myself in choosing field facilities (even if it means a lower profit margin). I want the best, though not necessarily the fanciest, and I expect to pay for it. If a facility's prices are out of line, we discuss it, but I don't believe in nickel-and-diming.

Finding the right fit: personal traits

Someone might be a good, even terrific, moderator, but are they right for a particular project? The characteristics of the moderator, both personal qualities and demographics, are important. However, it's not as simple as matching respondents' demographics (age, gender, ethnic group) to the moderator's. The guideline on moderator demographics is comfort: the moderator needs to be comfortable with the respondents and the topic; respondents need to be comfortable with the moderator.

Matching a moderator to respondents doesn't always work in predictable ways. Some clients assume that younger respondents are more comfortable with a moderator their own age, but it's not always the case. An older moderator who comes across as accepting, non-judgmental, and genuinely interested in a younger group's opinions may get much more than a contemporary who seems cold, superior, uptight, or competitive.

Some old stereotypes are simply not true

Some old stereotypes are simply not true. Women can interview men on financial, technical, and medical subjects. Men can interview women on shopping, household cleaning, and cosmetics. I once turned down a study that involved talking to men about "jock itch" after I'd completed a successful study where men talked freely to me about hemorrhoids. I figured that hemorrhoids can happen to either gender, so they could discuss it with a woman, but jock itch is as male as it gets. Even the male moderator I recommended for the study immediately recoiled at the topic. He said, "That's disgusting!" I never did have the chance to find out if men would have talked to me about jock itch, but a man uncomfortable with the subject probably wouldn't have been a better choice.

A good moderator makes use of personal similarities *or* differences from the group to mine information. Some moderator characteristics are obvious to the eye, while others are assumed or guessed at by respondents. Of course, there are many times when we are outsiders, but respondents may not realize it — they don't necessarily know where we're from, for instance.

A good

moderator

makes use of

personal

similarities or

differences

from the group

to mine

information

As an insider: A moderator similar to the group can convey understanding and sympathy. Insiders may need to find ways to encourage respondents to tell them what the group assumes they already know. *"This might seem obvious, but spell out for me why women . . .?"*

As an outsider: A moderator different from the group who is eager to understand will have respondents explain themselves. (*"What makes this appealing to men?" "What's it like to have a cat?" "I'm not a nurse, so please explain that to me."*) As a personal example, I don't have children, but because I'm a woman, mothers in my focus groups assume that I know about infant care. I emphasize that I've never had children and they need to tell me all about infant care in great detail, if that's what the project is about. Although I'm a confirmed cat lover, I have occasionally lied about it in pet projects, so that cat lovers feel that they have to help me understand why they adore these creatures.

Outsiders shouldn't be so outside that they alienate respondents, however. Part of the preparation for the "role" is being at least semi-knowledgeable about the subject and the respondents' world. When I interview nurses I may not know what a "step-down unit" is, but I have boned up on how their professional association works. I also consider it necessary to my work to read *People* magazine (homework I don't mind at all) so I am familiar with the names of pop culture stars and entertainment.

A good moderator knows how to be a chameleon, relating to people across the socio-economic spectrum by modifying dress, body language, and vocabulary. The sophisticated person who comes to your office might come across as more "down home" in a focus group. When a client asked me recently how I would deal with a group of teenage girls, for instance, I said that the most important element is to show respect for them, not to talk down by pretending to be up with the current lingo. Our job entails a certain amount of acting, of playing different roles.

There are limits to how far a moderator can stretch, of course, and certain mismatches can be serious mistakes. Some moderators may simply seem wrong to interview certain types of people, no matter how simpatico they are with the subject. A demographic match, especially in race and gender, between moderator and respondent is important when the issue is sensitive, such as a discussion about discrimination. Respondents should feel free to insult or criticize another group. A moderator who is "not like us" would be inhibiting. Someone with a pronounced New York accent might alienate people in the Deep South. Someone with a very theatrical manner may put off a staid conservative group. Appearance can become a barrier. A very thin moderator told me that when she did

A good moderator knows how to be a chameleon, relating to people across the socio-economic spectrum by modifying dress, body language, and vocabulary

focus groups with large-sized women about their self-perceptions several years ago, many respondents were hostile to her.

Advice to other moderators: do not attempt to do a project if you feel strongly that you would be wrong for it. Recently, I turned down a project studying cutting-edge ethnic urban teens about fashion. As a white woman whose middle name is not "hip," I didn't think I could build rapport with the group. It might have worked, but I didn't think it would be fair to the client, although it would have been a fascinating study. (I recommended an African-American moderator I know who is in his 50s; he may not be young, but he's cool.)

Finding the right fit: the category and topic

The moderator needs to be right for the client's category and the subject of the particular study. These may fit the moderator's personal background or interests (I love doing work for *The New York Times* in part because I have read the paper since I was a child) or, again, the moderator can prepare — up to a point. Conducting focus groups on topics that aren't naturals for me is fine if I feel I can achieve that level of semi-familiarity. I can do research on financial services, on computers, on medicine, if the study is not particularly technical. In fact, sometimes it's a plus that I'm not a maven in these fields. If I don't understand what the client is saying, very often the respondents won't either. Moderators who are very enthusiastic about high-tech can be biased in favor of the latest gizmos, one client told me. It was fine for me to do groups for *ESPN Magazine*, even though I am not a sports fan, because the study was about

A demographic match, especially in race and gender, between moderator and respondent is important when the issue is sensitive, such as a discussion about discrimination

the publication. If we had been talking about athletes and teams, though, I wouldn't have been the right moderator —I wouldn't have understood who the respondents were talking about and I probably would have asked dumb, irritating questions.

A moderator who has not done research on a product category can still have relevant experience for the project. Issues like advertising and packaging cut across categories, for instance. Sometimes, frankly, the client's desire for someone who has done exactly the same category before gets a little silly. The head of a research department at a well-known company once asked if I had ever done mascara research (a specialty, I guess). I hadn't, but I had moderated a number of focus groups on cosmetics. No, I didn't get the project.

What's the best choice if the topic is technical: the better researcher who will have to study the subject, or the specialist who isn't a top-level researcher? As long as the topic isn't extremely technical, I'd suggest going with the better researcher. To interview physicians, a pharmaceutical company used a moderator who specialized in medical research. Then they needed to interview consumers. The moderator was a disaster in that phase, because he rigidly followed the guide rather than probing responses, according to the ad agency researcher. Knowledge of medical language was irrelevant at this point. (Yes, I got the call for that project.)

Academic background can be relevant, of course. Good qualitative researchers come from a dazzling array of backgrounds that enrich our field. Psychology, the social sciences, and marketing are common, but there are excellent moderators who started life as actors or dentists. Psycho-

On technical topics, a good researcher may be a better choice as a moderator than a technical specialist

THE GOOD MODERATOR

- *Understands the client's values*
- *Is professional*
- *Catches on quickly*
- *Has creative suggestions*
- *Has insight*
- *Makes the client feel free to talk*
- *Listens*

Good qualitative researchers come from a dazzling array of backgrounds, including acting and dentistry; psychological insights aren't limited to psychologists

logical insights aren't limited to psychologists. Again, it comes back to the individual.

There's a trade-off between experience and freshness. Most clients like to use a "stable" of moderators (a term I particularly dislike) who get to know their product, organization, and needs. They don't have to brief the moderator from scratch for each project; the moderator's learning from one study is carried forward to the next. I prefer continuity, too, and not just because it's good for business. I feel I have a greater grasp of the subject and I like the sense of a relationship. We get to know the product's history, as well as the client's specific tastes, both on larger and smaller issues. (For one client who became upset when chicken was served at the focus groups because he had once witnessed his grandmother killing a bird, we had a note: "nothing that waddles or flies.") On the other hand, clients periodically want a different moderator who can look at things from a fresh perspective, with no vested interest in their prior insights. Increasing the size of that "stable" also makes sense since successful moderators may not be available when clients want them. At the extreme, there are some clients who do not seem to value continuity at all, constantly trying out different moderators for novelty. It's a risky strategy.

In addition to moderator/respondent rapport, there has to be rapport between moderator and client. Some of the qualities that make for a good moderator with respondents should be evident when clients talk with the researcher. The moderator understands what the client's values are and grasps what the client wants to accomplish in the particular project, comes across as professional, catches on quickly, has creative suggestions, has insight, makes the client feel free to talk, and, most importantly, listens.

MARKETING LINGO

Translating marketing-speak to real people language that the respondents and the moderator understand is essential. For example, one client urged me to find out what "aspirational images" to show about pain relief. What did this mean? Everyone wants to feel free of pain, to be their normal selves, but the client had something else in mind. Their real question was whether they should show the just-recovered sufferer being physically active or doing something more subdued. Another client wanted me to ask the group about "policy-setting" and "implementation" of a new office product. I didn't know what that meant. I doubt that the respondents would have known either. What this meant was using the product and putting some limits on how or when it was used by employees. In each case, I had to find out what these words meant to my clients. In the first case, "aspirational" meant that the client wanted to find out how people would feel after they'd used the product the advertising agency was marketing.

STEP 3: *Choose the right qualitative research technique*

For many clients, qualitative research means focus groups. Usually these are 2 hours long with 8 to 10 respondents. There are a number of variations: mini-groups (2 to 6 respondents), extended focus groups (2-$1/2$ to 4 hours) or shorter ones, supergroups (up to 20 respondents), telephone focus groups, and online focus groups, a relatively new development. There are individual depth interviews done in-person, by telephone or online. And currently in vogue is observational or ethnographic research, where people's behavior is studied wherever they would naturally be (e.g. in their homes, a bar, a store). All of these qualitative research techniques require many of the same skills and planning work that focus groups demand, but they also have special facilitation requirements of their own.

How do you know which type of qualitative research to choose? A number of factors play a role: the project schedule, the budget, the issue to be studied, and the type of respondents. Less talked about, but also important, are the researcher's style, personality, preferences, and even stamina. You can choose more than one method. If you decide to go with individual depth interviews, you can split interviews between moderators to get larger numbers or you can combine focus groups with one-on-ones, for example.

A full-size focus group (8 to 10 respondents) is useful when you want group interaction — for debate, to stimulate new ideas, and to observe word-of-mouth dynamics. If you are dealing with a sensitive subject, the group format can help respondents to open up when they realize that they share a problem such as a medical condition. (Other researchers feel individual interviews are essential for these subjects, but I disagree. The focus group tends to become something of a support group; respondents may share more with their peers than they do with a single interviewer.) It has become a cliché to say that respondents don't have much individual "air time" in a full focus group; the 2 hours divided by 10 respondents is only 12 minutes per person. In reality, respondents "express" their views not just when they are talking but in their body language. If one respondent makes a statement and the others vigorously nod, we've learned how several people feel at the same time.

The downside of full-sized focus groups is that they can be difficult to control. This is more of a problem with some groups than with others. Smaller sessions (6 to 8 respondents) tend to be better with executives or professionals discussing their field since these respondents want to express their views, often talk at length, and can be quite self-important. Ten little children in one group isn't ideal either. (See any similarities between the two types of respondents?) You can't always fill full-sized focus groups, and sometimes expense is an issue.

Mini-groups can include anywhere from 2 to 6 respondents. They are often "mini" in length as well—45 minutes to an hour. Certain studies simply don't require 2 hours. (Beware, however, of scheduling a group for an hour and then chocking it full of issues.) When there are just a few ads to show, for instance, it can be useful to conduct a series of mini-groups, rotating the order in which the ads are shown, to avoid the bias of an ad always being in a certain sequence. Mini-groups are also useful when budgets and schedules are tight. You can get more sessions in for less money and do these groups more quickly.

Sometimes the mini-group format is a matter of necessity—for example, when you can find only a few respondents who qualify for the study or the weather is horrible and only a few show up. Some clients set a minimum number of respondents for a focus group—6 or 7—but why not interview the people who come and learn something?

The problem with mini-groups is that they are only as

good as your respondents. There is a greater likelihood of being stuck with a difficult respondent in a small group. These groups can sometimes lack animation and they can end up being serial one-on-one interviews. "Dyads" and "triads" have become familiar terms (two or three respondents at a time), but, in my experience, there is nothing magical about them.

Mini-groups are

useful when

budgets and

schedules are

tight

One-on-one interviews (also called **Individual Depth Interviews,** or **IDIs**) are useful in several cases. They give respondents time to provide detailed anecdotal information on buying history or step-by-step decision-making. It may be good to avoid the focus group setting when there are strong concerns about group bias occurring or, for political reasons, when clients want to avoid possible internal debates about bias. IDIs are often used to explore advertising communication since, in the real world, people respond to ads on an individual basis. Sometimes respondents are so dissimilar demographically or in their attitudes that they would not be comfortable together. For a study of a medical device used by recovering heart patients and marathon runners, it would not have made sense to combine such disparate people. And unless you specifically want a debate, don't put pro-choice and anti-abortion supporters together.

There are several drawbacks with IDIs from both a research and practical standpoint. Sometimes respondents worry about pleasing the interviewer, or feel interrogated, even with a gentle interviewer. They nervously ask, "Is this what you're looking for?" There are no other respondents to play off, to agree or disagree with, to get ideas from. In-person IDIs can be grueling for both the moderator and the observers. One reason is that they tend to be less lively than focus groups. Another is that the schedules are often very long. To make the day productive, seven or eight hours of interviewing are often planned—on top of several hours of travel, an exhausting day or series of days. Here's where moderator personality comes into play. There are many moderators who enjoy depth interviews, but I dislike such day-long schedules, although I can do the same number of hours of focus groups without fatigue.

One-on-ones in person or by phone?

In this supposedly high-tech era, it is interesting that nearly all qualitative research is still done face-to-face. The moderator and, typically, the clients travel sometimes thousands of miles to see and listen to consumers.

If use of the telephone seems almost old-fashioned compared with the Internet, it's notable that until only recently there was a lot of resistance to conducting qualitative research by phone.

Talking with and observing respondents firsthand is extremely valuable, but are there situations where it is just as effective, or even preferable, to conduct interviews by telephone or by other "virtual" means?

The answer is yes and no. Telephone interviews are commonplace for quantitative research and executive-level depth interviews. This has become a routine way of contacting professionals and business executives who are difficult to recruit for in-person interviews at a facility (or even in their offices where they are frequently interrupted). At the same time, there is an assumption that

It may be good to avoid the focus group setting when there are strong concerns about group bias occurring or, for political reasons, when clients want to avoid possible internal debates about bias

Telephone interviews have become a routine way of contacting professionals and business executives who are difficult to recruit

consumers cannot be interviewed in-depth by phone. Why this contradiction?

Conventional wisdom is that executives are accustomed to talking on the phone, but that "ordinary" consumers are not. The perception is that consumers can be asked multiple-choice questions on the phone, along with a few brief open-ends ("Why do you say that?" "What do you like/not like about X?"), but they would be uncomfortable talking over the phone in any greater depth about their thoughts and feelings.

In fact, most consumers have long been accustomed to conducting personal and business relationships over the telephone—and telephone interviews can be an excellent alternative or supplement to the face-to-face methods of qualitative research.

We have conducted a good number of telephone interview studies, ranging in length from 20 minutes to an hour and with sample sizes from 25 up to 250 respondents, a very large number for qualitative research. Virtually all of the questions were open-ended, with interviewers probing responses. Some studies included closed-ends as well (such as ratings). This combination of qualitative and quantitative research gives clients insights (the whys) along with some numbers (how many).

Telephone interviews offer several advantages over in-person interviews. They are a good way to interview people around the country rather than in just one or two markets, providing a broader picture of consumers and businesspeople. Phone interviews save time since no travel is required and there is no "dead time" spent waiting for respondents to arrive at a facility. They save money—not just on travel, but on recruiting and cooperation fees. In studies where only a brief interview is needed (under half an hour), why bring respondents into a facility if it's not necessary? Phone interviews also save energy for interviewer and client. Interviewers feel fresher and more alert working from their home or office, where they can relax between interviews. This, in turn, can improve the quality of the interviews. Sometimes it simply isn't possible to recruit enough respondents for focus groups in any one market, so phone interviews are a good alternative. A medical device manufacturer wanted to interview recent purchasers who had sent in warranty cards, for instance, but there were only about 100 names nationwide. Phone interviews solved the problem.

There are times when using the phone is even preferable to in-person interviews. Respondents are in their own home or office, the environment where they use the product being discussed. In a study of a cable channel, when one woman said her daughter had been the real reason she subscribed, it was possible to get the daughter on the phone to find out what had really happened. Sometimes it's even an advantage that the respondent can't see the interviewer. Not knowing what that person looks like

When the objective is to spark new ideas, build on a concept, or explore a category or lifestyle, the in-person focus group retains its importance

There are several keys to making phone depth interviews work:

- Pre-scheduled appointments
- Honesty about the interview length
- Generous respondent incentives ($1 per minute for mainstream consumers is a good rule of thumb)
- Top level interviewers who are true focus group moderators, not ordinary phone interviewers
- Flexibility in interviewing, starting with easy, non-threatening questions

(heavy/thin, older/younger, sophisticated/mainstream)can be liberating, taking away concerns about offending or pleasing. A frequent business traveler talking about the importance of a female flight attendant's appearance was not inhibited by knowing my age or looks, for instance.

Several additional benefits are possible. Transcripts of the phone interviews can also be delivered within a few days, since we type as we go. This is considerably faster than for focus groups in most cases. Audiotaping is possible on studies with respondents who can't be recognized individually by the client, preserving their anonymity. With digital recording, a "sound bite" tape can be put together to give clients "the voice of the consumer." Materials can also be sent to respondents in advance or, via fax and online, during the interview.

Depth interviews—in-person, by phone, or online—will not replace focus groups, I believe. When the objective is to spark new ideas, build on a concept, or explore a category or lifestyle, the in-person focus group retains its importance. In-person interviews will still be wanted when the client needs to see and hear the respondents first-hand.

The interviewer digs out the who-what-where in individual interviews:

- Where were you then?
- Why did you use the product?
- What did you feel like before using it?
- Who else was there and what did they do or say?
- How did you feel during and after using the product?
- What was the setting?
- What was going on? What did the place look like?
- How were you dressed?

However, telephone interviews should not be rejected out of hand. Under the right circumstances, they can be a valuable addition to the consumer research repertoire.

Telephone focus groups are used by some market research companies. (I have participated in a few, but we do not provide this service.) Used more for executive interviews, phone focus groups can bring together geographically scattered professionals in specialized fields like medicine or telecommunications. Special equipment is needed for the teleconferencing; an assistant can talk directly to individual respondents in privacy, asking them, for instance, to speak up or to say less. Because participants, including the moderator, typically don't know one another, respondents are asked to start each comment by identifying themselves ("This is Cindi. I love the product."). This can be somewhat stilted. It is also harder for clients to follow individual respondents through the interview.

STEP 4: *Define the task*

There are roadblocks to a well-designed project that may appear in the task definition phase. One common situation is when there's a stated task, but there's another agenda that may be more important.

An example: When I was called in to do a study for a national magazine, I was initially told they wanted to do groups because they were disappointed in their level of new subscriptions. Midway through the project, I found out that the long-time editor was going to be leaving soon and that no successor had been named. The major reason for these focus groups was, in fact, to get some new direction for the magazine: What did fans want continued and

Sometimes it requires some detective work to find out what the real goal of the research is

what might attract new readers? The moral of the story is that sometimes it requires some detective work to find out what the real goal of the research is. Following the original goal, I would have focused on what might bring in more readers. Knowing the second, real goal, I focused more on understanding what might change about the magazine.

That's not to say that focus groups can't work on two goals at once. An example: I did a study for another magazine where the editor had the goal of finding out what subscribers thought of her magazine. The publisher had another: To come up with great sound bites ("good tape") to show advertisers what a desirable audience the magazine had.

Moderators always need to find out what the client's current situation is, even if it seems to be outside the scope of the project

Not being informed about the real objectives is a hindrance to the researcher and, unfortunately, it happens too often. Sometimes the client intentionally withholds information to avoid "biasing" the researcher. Sometimes the client doesn't seem to realize that the moderator would benefit by knowing what is really going on. Once, at the very end of a series of focus groups, during the debrief, a food client casually mentioned that the names I had been asking about for a line of vegetables would be used for a broader line of foods. This not only changed the way we analyzed what we heard, it meant that we never had the opportunity to interview respondents on the true issue of the research.

Moderators always need to find out what the company or organization's current situation is, even if it seems to be outside the narrow scope of the research project. Here are some questions that might be asked at the beginning of a study.

Asking the client basic questions can be an important first step:

- What's the reason you want to do the research?

- Why are you doing this study now?

- What is it you want to learn? Why do you want to learn it? How will you use the information — what kinds of decisions or steps will you be considering?

- How is the product doing — is it successful, is it having problems?

- What guesses do you have about the source of the problems?

- Who do you think your current customers are? Your competitors?

- What strategies do you use to talk to current customers?

- What kinds of people do you think are potential customers?

- What strategies do you use to attract new customers?

- What's the marketing background of the product/brand? What has been done in the past that worked or didn't work?

- Can you show me past advertising? Past research?

- How is your product actually different from competitors' or customers' perceptions?

Focus groups have two different missions:

DIAGNOSTIC: This is the most common type of study. An organization has a problem or objective and the purpose of the research is to figure out a diagnosis. The client wants to hear the truth no matter how much it hurts.

PROMOTIONAL: The research is intended to communicate a certain point to the client's end customer. A manufacturer wants to show retailers that consumers like its new product; a magazine wants advertisers to see what great readers it has and how much they love the publication.

STEP 5: *Design the project* _____

Getting the project design right in the beginning means that the study will have value and credibility at the end

The design of the project will guide you throughout the process. Getting it right in the beginning means that the study will have value and credibility at the end. When someone calls my office and asks for focus groups, I often take them through a diagnostic process to figure out how many focus groups they'll need, what kinds of people should be interviewed, where the groups should be held — or even if they need focus groups at all. Clients familiar with focus group research often have all of that figured out ahead of time even before they call me, and just want to talk about the topic guide and screening. However, if their design doesn't make sense to me, I view it as part of my role as "qualitative research consultant" to raise issues for them to think about.

The decision on the number and location of the focus groups brings together budget realities, logistics, and research considerations. Six to eight groups is typically considered a good number, especially for a broad-ranging study of attitudes and usage or a study of lifestyles. Usually there is some geographic variety (two groups per market with markets in different regions); different segments of consumers or businesspeople interviewed. Several possible market splits are: established versus new; strong competition versus weak; urban, suburban, rural. A minimum of two groups per market is best.

To save money and time, and to encourage the marketing team to observe, clients often want only one day of interviewing (two to three groups) at a relatively nearby facility. If the purpose of the research is to get feedback on some new concepts, that may be fine. Staying in the hometown area can be a mistake sometimes, however. New Yorkers should get out of Manhattan, which is representative of no market other than itself. Doing research in a small company-dominated town where the client is headquartered has obvious biases.

On the one extreme, it is virtually never a good idea to conduct just one focus group on a subject. A single group gives observers the false impression that they know a topic; even with two sessions, we can see if the reactions are similar or just a fluke. It is especially alarming when a client asks for one group in order to make a serious decision. We have refused to do this in several cases.

At the other extreme, few topics justify a large number of focus groups (16+) in the U.S. alone, even if the client can afford it. Financially remunerative though these may be, we usually advise against doing so many groups. The exceptions are when several very different segments need to be studied, when it is politically important for the client to go a variety of markets, or when the project has multiple phases (e.g., first broad exploratory, then reactions to concepts). The danger in such large studies is that the client thinks this is quantitative research with numbers even though the topics covered changed. The learning curve also drops off sharply for the researcher and the client who no longer hears anything new.

The choice of markets should be tailored to the client's issues. For a national study, usually it is wise to include the four basic regions: East Coast, West Coast, South, Midwest. If the budget allows only three regions, the decision should be based on where the product or category is strong. Depending on the client's product, a "typical" or "leading edge" market within the region may be appropriate. If the

Doing only one focus group gives observers the false impression that they know a topic

If the budget allows only three regions, the decision should be based on where the product or category is strong

product is aimed at trendsetters, go to the coasts, picking more "hip" markets. In addition, consider doing one or two markets elsewhere to see if the trend is spreading or has potential. The types of respondents dictate certain markets, too. If you are looking for certain industries or certain demographic groups, go where they are. (Sounds obvious, but too often clients pick a market and ask for an ethnic group that is only a small proportion of residents there.) Some markets may be inappropriate for a project. For example, there are not enough of the kind of people the client wants (such as households with $100,000+ incomes) or the market is headquarters of the client's competition (don't go to Atlanta to study soft drinks, or St. Louis to study beer). The market may be dominated by an industry where respondents will be screened out for security reasons (insurance companies in Hartford, Connecticut). There may be some other characteristic peculiar to that market that is a problem (too many military people in San Diego or Jacksonville buying at the PX, not regular stores). Logistical considerations also come into play. Certain markets in a region have better facilities or are easier to travel to than others. Avoiding markets during seasonal weather problems makes sense. Sometimes the client wants to visit

---

There are three key reasons for separating focus groups demographically:

■ To allow for respondents' comfort level on sensitive or intimate issues

■ To give respondents the freedom to speak freely about people not in the room

■ To give the moderator and client the opportunity to observe and compare groups for a clear perception of their differences

a relative. (As long as this doesn't sacrifice the research purpose, why not?)

Composition of the groups is another key issue in study design. Should all the groups be the same in terms of respondent type or should they be divided? And, if they are divided, on what basis? In some projects, especially smaller ones, the respondent requirements are the same across sessions. For instance, in a study of sheets and pillowcases, all respondents were women who had made purchases in the past year.

Clearly, there is no need to separate groups on every dimension. Instead, a decision has to be made on what variable is most important.

Here again, the rule of two is a good one: have at least two sessions per "cell" or type of respondent. That means two groups with the client's users compared with two groups of past users, and two groups of prospects who have never used the product (one of each type in a market).

Don't go to Atlanta to study soft drinks, or St. Louis to study beer

What's the hypothesis?

It's typical to make an outline of questions to be asked in the study. To get more out of the research, though, it's important to identify some possible ideas to explore. Don't fall in love with these ideas; just use them to find out more.

Interview the client. If the company is having problems, what are the managers' hypotheses or hunches about the source—the absence of advertising, conflicting messages, a product problem? In a study of employee turnover, for instance, a major company thought ethnic discrimination was probably a key issue. When this didn't come up spontaneously in the interview, we directly asked about it. To the client's surprise, past employees felt this was the least of the company's problems.

Look at the previous research, qualitative and/or quantitative. This research may or may not be current, useful, or even well done, but it will bring up ideas to explore. These studies also reveal what the client knows already, and what will be new information. However, clients are often reluctant to hand over reports because they don't want to "bias" the moderator. A good researcher, of course, will not be biased. In fact, the moderator may be inspired to extend the learning of the previous research.

Interview yourself. Moderators have the advantage of being company outsiders, which means they may see things as ordinary civilians do, as opposed to staff members. When a client shows me materials for a study and I don't understand them, I speak up. There's a chance the respondents won't understand either and the client may want to modify the materials. (A list of slogans for a financial services client included the phrase "protect your assets." My immediate association was "cover your tushie." Guess what? A respondent said the same thing!)

Get to know the product — go shopping to see it on the shelves next to competition (if you can even locate it in the store), read a year's worth of issues, watch the television program, etc. Doing the homework is essential for understanding the product and, in turn, developing hypotheses to explore. Often, the product is very different from what we had thought beforehand, or from the way respondents perceive it.

Speaking of bias, moderators need to be honest with themselves about their own hypotheses and feelings. Bias can affect both the interview process (what is and isn't asked, how it's asked) and the analysis. Many of the products and services that I research are ones that I use, so I have personal feelings, sometimes strong ones. Not using a product or brand can entail bias, too, if the researcher sees the client's product negatively.

In addition to personal bias, there's intellectual bias — when the researcher has the problem figured out before even walking into the research facility, has the report written in reality or mentally after the first few groups. If the moderator has worked on the product before, it may be tempting to support ideas discovered in previous studies.

Bias can be personal, intellectual, or political

When I was starting out in the 1970s, I observed focus groups about cold medicine moderated by a man I worked with. The women complained that when their husbands got sick, they were "big babies" who demanded to be taken care of. However, when the women got sick, they said there was no one there to tend to their needs; instead, they still had to look after their children and husband. The moderator made the judgment that women have a martyr complex — on some level, they enjoyed the situation. Wasn't it also possible that the women's complaints were genuine, that their description of what happened in their lives was true?

One of the biggest sources of potential bias is, of course, the desire to please the client. In the worst instance, a moderator may just play back what a client wants to hear — respondents thought the product was incredibly wonderful or they thought it was totally stupid (some clients actually want negative findings). If clients like the results, they often like the moderator and vice versa, the old "shoot-the-messenger" with bad news problem. More subtly, it can be difficult to interpret the research without thinking of the

Moderators

quickly lose

credibility if

they just cater

to the clients;

they get respect

for telling

people things

that they may

not want to

hear

client's biases. With so many people attending the focus groups, there may be many factions to please: the market research people (who usually hire the moderator) see things one way, the marketing people another, the agency yet another. Moderators quickly lose credibility if they just cater to the clients; they get respect for telling people things that they may not want to hear. In addition to our sense of integrity and pride, I really believe it's in our best business interest to be honest about what the research seems to mean.

The most difficult struggle in striving to be objective, however, is when deeply held philosophical beliefs come into play. For instance, I'm a feminist, and there are times when I may have to report what I consider to be disappointing things about women — that they feel or act in a way that I don't think is particularly feminist. But, of course, I do report it because that is my job. It's easier when I work on a project that I don't really have passion about either way. It usually doesn't matter to me personally which packaging color respondents prefer — blue and green are both okay with me.

Managing expectations

The beginning of a project is a good time to manage clients' expectations, especially those staff members new to the focus group process. You have to tell them that they may hear and see things in the group that they won't like. They may hear people being critical of their work; they may find that people who are their customers aren't as smart or sophisticated or as beautiful as they envision. This is tough on the corporate — and sometimes individual — ego. It's important to find tactful ways of reminding people to stay open-minded. At the same time, it's important to be sensitive to what your clients feel when they are in that back room, listening to consumers tear apart something they may have spent months or even years working on. People's jobs can be on the line; if an ad agency loses an account, many people's jobs may be lost.

Some other researchers give a speech in the back room about the right and wrong way to listen to the groups. I don't like lecturing people, so I don't do that. If I know that someone is brand new to qualitative research, I do take more time explaining what to expect.

Sometimes, focus groups are tough on the corporate ego

By managing expectations, the moderator may head off the tendency of viewers to blame negative respondent comments on the recruiting or on the moderator. Throughout the process, if you remain conscious of the "ouch factor" when a particularly bitter truth comes out, it may help to remind the client that it's all part of the learning and improvement process. It may not feel good at the moment, but it'll help later. And that's what it's really about.

CHAPTER 4

Managing Field Work

> There are more problems with mistakes than with cheating. There's an incentive to cheat because we put pressure on our suppliers to get people there at the groups; there's pressure on the recruiters to get people or they'll be fired. Sometimes that pressure is unrealistic. But **cheating is not rampant.** Still moderators have to work with the field to help them to have good procedures, good databases.
>
> —*Jim Bryson*
> Qualitative Research Consultants Association,
> President, and President of Research Concepts and
> 20/20 Research and QualTalk.com

THE FIELD SERVICE INDUSTRY in the U.S. has, quite literally, climbed out of the basement. Focus groups used to be conducted in the kitchens and dens of the field supervisors' homes.

I remember several particularly uncomfortable projects. In one, clients had to sit on hard metal chairs in the supervisor's den among her husband's many dental publications. In another, a discussion on stomach remedies held in a basement was interrupted by the slurping sounds of the supervisor's dog drinking out of the toilet, reminding respondents of their own rumbling tummies.

When one-way mirror facilities started coming in, they were generally primitive. One field service had a wall of framed mirrors, pretending to be a living room and hoping respondents didn't catch on to the viewing. The clients had a strange broken-up picture of the respondents. Another had the viewing room at the back of the focus group room with a partition that did not reach the ceiling, so clients were held captive in complete silence for the entire session.

What a difference today! What was a mom-and-pop operation has become big business. A number of corporate chains are opening up more and more facilities around the country. Modern facilities are often large, well-appointed, and even glamorous. They typically have multiple rooms. One of these is often a small interviewing room for one-on-ones, which is both less expensive and less intimidating to the respondent. Equipment like VCRs to show commercials is commonplace.

Many back rooms today are built for 20 observers, often theater-style with stepped-up levels for better viewing. There are adjoining lounges with phones and closed-circuit TV for viewing; the lights can be left on here, unlike the room behind the mirror. Some have booths so clients and moderators can make private calls because the facility is their office-on-the-road. A video camera on a tripod or attached to the ceiling is used for stationary recording in many facilities. Well-stocked refrigerators are commonplace, some with beer and wine. Assorted executive toys are offered by some facilities, often labeled with the company's name. Visiting qualitative researchers and clients appreciate the comfort, comment on amenities, and often choose field services based on their attractiveness.

Client food has become more elaborate than the early days of cold cuts only. An array of ethnic dinner choices is now standard; one facility ran an ad a few years ago bragging that it offered sushi. Back rooms are typically stuffed with candy and junk foods; weight gain is a side effect of

What was a

mom–and–pop

operation has

become big

business

CONFERENCE ROOM OR LIVING ROOM?

In a number of countries, focus groups are often still conducted in private homes, out of necessity or choice. In the United Kingdom, for instance, there are a growing number of viewing "studios," but many British researchers insist that the living room environment is the best in making respondents feel comfortable. They disapprove of what they see as the sterility of U.S. facilities. I don't agree, at least for groups done in the States. When I've done focus groups in a "living room" setting (a real home or facility), I found that strangers squooshed onto a sofa together did not seem comfortable physically or psychologically. It is also difficult to control the inevitable side conversations. I didn't think respondents were any more open than they are in a facility. On certain subjects, like ones concerning aesthetic taste, it may be preferable to be in a neutral-looking conference room than a personally decorated home.

focus group viewing. M&Ms™ are the candy of choice, often joked about in the industry. Some clients specify which type of M&Ms they want—and they aren't kidding.

Each year, the level of what is considered standard in a facility seems to go up a notch. With improvements in technology, the following equipment is becoming more commonplace: outlets for computer note-taking at each client seat in the back room, computers clients can use for revising materials, Internet access in both the respondent and back rooms (for showing websites to respondents, checking e-mail for clients), and LCD projectors for showing websites. A new addition at one facility is an LCD readout in the back room showing which respondents (by number on the spreadsheets) have arrived for the focus group.

In major markets like New York and Chicago, there are a number of large well-appointed facilities within blocks of one another. It has become relatively easy, too, to find one or two field services with a focus group room facility in the top-20 markets. At the opposite end, small markets and rural areas, which are used less often in market research, may have archaic facilities or none at all. In these cases, focus groups are sometimes run in a local hotel with clients observing via closed-circuit hook-up in a room next door. If there are only one or two clients and they promise to keep a poker face throughout the sessions, they can sit in the back of the focus group room.

Bigger isn't always better for you

This trend to more professional facilities is helpful, but certain aspects are irritating and get in the way of good research. In some multi-room facilities, respondents have to wait in either cavernous waiting areas or cramped ones, both of which make them feel ill at ease. It is difficult for the facility assistants to check everyone in and out at the same time for several different sessions. Big isn't better in the case of oversize conference tables. Side conversations inevitably occur at a large table, it's difficult to hear the respondents at the opposite end, and respondents, literally, feel more remote from the process. In some larger facilities, the back room is a long distance from the conference room —the moderator has to sprint around to find out what the client wants.

Some physical aspects of facilities to consider

A good facility helps moderators by providing a physical set-up that lets them select appropriate respondents for the group, communicate well with respondents and clients, and present materials during the sessions. Here are some specifics for a well-designed facility:

- **Location** — in an area that is convenient to recruit the respondents desired on a particular project (affluent, downscale, etc.); one that is safe, both in perception and reality; in a building without noisy neighbors (we've struggled to do groups next to nightclubs, under a bowling alley, and beneath a ballroom dance studio).

- **Parking area and facility entrance** — clearly marked so respondents feel comfortable right from the beginning. There should be enough parking spaces, also clearly identified, in a well-lit area close to the building.

- **Separate entrance for clients** — so clients don't troop in right in front of respondents. This helps to preserve client anonymity, often not revealed until the end of the session, sometimes not disclosed at all. Seeing a gaggle of clients, all dressed in fashionable black, or a well-known editor, for instance, could cause some discomfort and inhibition among respondents. How can they say they hate the magazine when they know the editor is listening?

- **Waiting room** — especially important in creating the right environment from the start. The check-in desk should be immediately visible to respondents as they enter the facility. The waiting room should be large enough to accommodate all of the respondents expected for all rooms; none should have to stand around awkwardly. This area should also have enough room for refreshments, a good way to make people feel welcome. Moderators often prefer that respondents eat their dinners before the groups, removing a distraction from the sessions. I like

THE WAITING ROOM

- ▶ *Prominent check-in desk*
- ▶ *Adequate seating*
- ▶ *Refreshments available*
- ▶ *Separate waiting rooms for different focus groups*
- ▶ *Prevent respondents from seeing observers or overhearing the subject in advance*

separate waiting rooms for different focus groups. This seems more personal than the huge bullpen and prevents confusion later about who goes where. (I was once sent the wrong group of respondents.) It's especially helpful to have respondents wait outside the conference room of a different client so they don't see their observers or overhear the subject of their group in advance.

Good temperature control — an important feature unfortunately overlooked at many facilities. There should be controls in both the conference and back room, not in the hall somewhere. When one control works for both rooms, inevitably either the respondents or the clients are miserable. A good system is needed that doesn't swing from freezing to hot. Too often I have to jump up several times in a session to make adjustments when I see respondents hugging themselves to keep warm or yawning from the stuffiness (of the room, not the discussion). The air-conditioning system needs to be quiet so it doesn't drown out the tapes. A back-up set of good old-fashioned electrical fans is a good idea since air conditioning doesn't always work.

High-quality audio and videotape — absolutely essential. This means using good-quality equipment and tapes that are checked at the start of each day's work. There have been too many disasters with tapes not recording. An extra tape recorder on the conference table—a small one, not a giant boom box that dominates the respondents' view— provides extra insurance. When a video camera is built in, it should be positioned to capture as many faces as possible. One facility had two cameras, one at each side of the mirror. This set-up was great when an operator in another room cut back and forth for close-ups, but it was a disaster for stationary recording when just one camera was selected. It left out the faces of half the group!

Conference tables — the places where respondents sit are very important to respondent comfort. The huge tables at many facilities today can seem overwhelming and distancing. My first step when I arrive is often to see if they are modular and I can take a section away. Ideally, the table should be able to be modified in size so it can handle larger or smaller focus groups. Scaled-down furniture adds to the comfort of children in their groups. For "super groups" with a larger number of respondents and more free-wheeling format, moderators may want to get rid of the conference table all together.

The back room — this should be designed to facilitate client viewing. If that sounds obvious, keep in mind that one of the main reasons clients decide they won't come back to a facility is a cramped or otherwise uncomfortable back room. The size of the room is critical since there are often 15 to 20 clients observing, and they do not want to be on top of each other. Theater or stadium seating in rows makes it easier to get a good view. Some facilities have a set of individual round tables scattered around the room on one level; although this is less like school and gives clients more room to spread out, it is more difficult for viewing. Typically, the mirror is straight across the room, an arrangement that works well, but some facilities have odd-shaped rooms with mirrors along two angled walls, a set-up that gives at least some viewers a distorted view. Hooded lighting over

THE BACK ROOM

- ▶ *Large enough for 15 to 20 clients*
- ▶ *Theater or stadium seating in rows*
- ▶ *One level seating is more difficult for viewing*
- ▶ *The mirror straight across the room*
- ▶ *Hooded lighting over the tables/desks*
- ▶ *Electrical outlets throughout the room*
- ▶ *Comfortable chairs*
- ▶ *Hot plates to keep refreshments warm*
- ▶ *Entrance lighting*

the tables/desks makes it possible for observers to take notes yet doesn't show through the mirror. Also needed are electrical outlets throughout the room for clients' computers; chairs that are comfortable but not too huge so the room doesn't get cramped; and of course, room for refreshments with hot plates to keep food warm. (I'm constantly surprised by the fact that even the most fancy facilities stint on small items like hot plates.) Lighting or glow-in-the-dark strips on the stairs are absent from a number of facilities. One of my clients once fell and broke an ankle in the dark.

Sound proofing—between the conference and back rooms, as well as between the conference and waiting rooms. A solid one-way mirror prevents respondents from hearing clients. Even when clients are asked to keep their voices low, they may laugh at some respondent comments. "Are they laughing at us?" one respondent asked. Or clients may make cracks about the comments. One audibly exclaimed, "Says you!" Furthermore, you don't want respondents who are waiting for the next group to be influenced by hearing what's going on in the session. Most important, competitors using the same facility shouldn't hear confidential information from other sessions.

Sound proofing: "Are they laughing at us?"

Good lighting in the conference room. Lighting in the best facilities can be adjusted to several different levels — brighter for videotaping, lower for showing videos or LCD slides. If the overhead lights are turned out completely while respondents look at a commercial, for instance, clients can't observe respondents' faces. Were they smiling or sitting grimly?

What's my dream facility? What I'd really love is a shower and a sofa after a long flight to help me get refreshed for the hours of work ahead!

Field service selection

The importance of the physical set-up from the respondent's point of view cannot be emphasized enough

Two key factors determine which field service to use for focus groups: the quality of the recruiting and the physical set-up of the facility. In the U.S., recruiting and facilities are usually bundled together, although this is not true in a number of other countries. Definitely the most important factor in selection is the recruiting. If the respondents are not the type of people needed for the project, the study will be useless. However, if a facility is rundown or cramped, clients will be unhappy, no matter how good the recruiting. As a result, we sometimes select a better space and work with an independent recruiter.

The quality of the field service is so important that it can even play a role in deciding where to conduct the focus groups. In some cases, clients must go to certain cities if, for instance, that's where their stores are or a test market is underway. In other cases, there's some flexibility, so markets can be chosen based on where the best field services are. Sometimes we've had bad experiences or negative word-of-mouth about a market so we'll suggest avoiding it.

The importance of the physical set-up from the respondent's point of view also cannot be emphasized enough. With the concern of field services about the client's comfort, the respondent is often overlooked. First-time respondents, in particular, typically arrive with some anxiety, needing reassurance. If the physical setting is awkward, uncomfortable, cold — literally and figuratively — the best qualitative researcher will have a struggle to establish and maintain rapport.

The Qualitative Research Consultants Association (QRCA) is an invaluable resource in selecting field services. The City List, available only to members and updated annually, shows which members have been to which markets in the six months before they filled in the form. Members can then contact other moderators to get their frank opinions. We've used this service often if we're going somewhere new or haven't been happy with a facility in the past.

Choosing a field service solely on price is a mistake. What's the point of saving money if the quality of recruiting is bad or if too few or no respondents show up for the groups? If a field service has done good work for us, we go back. Developing a good relationship with a service pays off. Its managers often go out of their way to give us their better rooms, to nudge another client to see if dates are available, and so on. In addition, they know how we like to do things. If a field service is out of line in price in its market, it may be open to bringing the price down.

When you're selecting a facility out of several in a market, go back to the purpose of the study. Is the facility conveniently located to recruit the respondents you want — certain ethnic groups, income groups, businesses, the people on your client's list? Most facilities today are in office buildings; these have a professional image that many respondents, especially business people, find reassuring. Mall facilities aren't used very much anymore for focus groups but they work well if the session entails a visit to a store.

CONTACT INFORMATION

The Qualitative Research Consultants Association (QRCA)
P.O. Box 2396
Gaithersburg, MD 20886-2396
toll free:
888-674-7722
fax:
301-391-6281
email:
qrca@qrca.org

Conference room set-up ——————————————————

The conference room is where the real work of the research goes on. The room should be set up in a way that, again, makes the respondents comfortable and enables the moderator to do the job, such as presenting materials. Interestingly, moderators seem to have a number of different ideas on what is best. One reason I get to facilities early is to rearrange furniture and double check that I have everything I need. Often, even in facilities I use repeatedly, changes need to be made.

This is what I consider minimum equipment in a conference room:

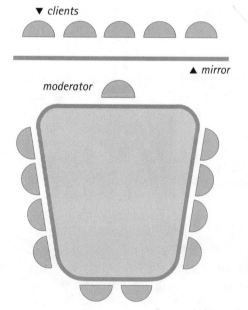

▼ *clients*

▲ *mirror*

moderator

A modified trapezoid conference table shape is best, with the widest point at the end near the mirror so clients can see the faces of all respondents. The most commonly used table shape is a regular rectangle with the narrow end facing the camera, headed by the moderator, which makes full viewing of all respondents impossible. Weird, distracting table shapes should be avoided. One facility used to have an octagonal modular table with a hole in the center. This not only created problems when we needed to put things on the table, it led to the unfortunate situation of drawing people's attention to one another's feet.

At least one good easel with a full pad of paper and a number of markers in different colors that are not all dried out. Additional easels may be needed if the focus group breaks into smaller groups.

Chairs that are well padded—it's hard to sit for two hours! In addition, chairs with arms take up too much room. Chairs should not swivel, and they must not squeak. It's very distracting. The moderator's chair should either be the same size as the respondents' or only slightly larger. A "throne" is not good because it literally places the moderator on a superior level.

A ledge on all the non–mirrored walls for displaying materials, wide enough that poster boards can stand up properly. Pushpins and masking tape should be handy.

Tablecloths and drop cloths to cover materials until respondents are supposed to see them.

A small table near the moderator for pads and pencils that will be handed out to respondents as well as materials that will be shown during the sessions.

A separate table for beverages. I like to have cookies and fruit with plates and napkins right on the conference table, handy for respondents. They can walk over to get the beverages, which take up too much room on the conference table.

Extra tables available if the study entails showing lots of materials.

> **THE CONFERENCE ROOM**
> ▶ *Sturdy easels*
> ▶ *Comfortable chairs*
> ▶ *Display ledge*
> ▶ *Separate tables for materials, refreshments, supplies, and displays*
> ▶ *Drop cloths*
> ▶ *Tapered conference table*

Set-up don'ts

Every aspect of the physical set-up should make respondents feel welcome and respected. Many facilities forget this. Here's a brief list of set-ups that are fairly standard at facilities around the United States but, I believe, get in the way of an effective process. Despite our detailed instructions to the contrary, many facilities arrange the conference room this way:

Setting the table with one respondent chair at the end facing the moderator. This implies that there is a leader among the respondents, while placing two or three seats opposite the moderator makes all the respondents equals.

Pads and pencils at each respondent's place at the table. This looks too much like school to me. If I were a respondent, I would wonder if I'm supposed to take notes. I immediately take these away, putting them on a table near me, and hand them out when needed later on.

No moderator name card. This is another small touch that is important in creating rapport. Respondents usually have table tent cards with their names written on both sides so the moderator and other respondents can see them. So why shouldn't the moderator? The moderator is an intentionally neutral person who reveals little about his personal life, but having a name is essential to communicate, "I want you to feel comfortable and to share with me."

Few or no refreshments. A number of moderators don't provide any refreshments in the room, because it costs money or they think it's a distraction. Facilities also resist our instructions to put beverages and food inside the room or they only put some of what we want there. It's hard to sit in a room for two hours without something to drink, especially when the focus group takes place around mealtime. Even though we're paying respondents to be there, they are doing us a favor by giving their time and sharing their insights. Food is a critical part of

The moderator is an intentionally neutral person who reveals little about her personal life— but giving your name is essential for rapport

creating a welcoming atmosphere, I believe. It helps people to relax and open up; it's a non-verbal way of showing respect. A respondent in a recent focus group thanked us for having refreshments. She had attended a three-hour group without any and reported that respondents rebelled in an exodus to the vending machines.

The selection of food and beverages is also important. The typical assortment, if there's anything, is cookies, regular coffee, carbonated soft drinks (often just colas) and a pitcher of water. We like to add some fruit and bottled water as well as decaffeinated coffee, especially for evening groups. These additions give health- and weight-conscious respondents a choice. There is truth to the argument that food can be a distraction. A simple way of handling this is to spread the food, plates, and napkins around the table so respondents don't have to reach across the table or ask someone else to pass a plate. Fruit should be finger food, not grapes on a huge bunch or apples no one wants to carve. No potato chips; they're just too noisy. Now, if only someone could invent soft ice cubes that wouldn't bang in glasses!

Food and beverages should give health- and weight-conscious respondents a choice

_____ Recruiting: the core of quality fieldwork

The most important part of the field service's job is getting the recruiting right: finding the type of respondents the client is looking for, making sure a desired number show up and that they come on time. It isn't as easy as it sounds. Clients can spend a lot of time and money on air travel only to get to a facility and find that just one or two respondents showed up for a group that was supposed to have eight to ten people. When unforeseen situations beyond the field service's control occur (a big traffic tie-up, delayed flights, a storm), the moderator and the field service have to work together to deal with these situations. Most of all, the field service and moderator need to communicate well on the screening process.

THE CHEATER/REPEATER/DECEIVER

An important issue in qualitative research is what QRCA calls the Cheater/Repeater/Deceiver issue—respondents who, respectively, pretend to be people they aren't (in demographics, product usage), "professionals" who go to focus groups regularly, and recruiters who, at the very least, nudge respondents into fudging their qualifications. Over the years, several clients have told me they personally know people who supplement their living by attending focus groups. Some people I know have said recruiters helped them get into groups they didn't belong in. ("Tell them you live in Manhattan, not Brooklyn." "You spent around $200 on business shirts last year, didn't you?") Some recruiters reportedly instruct the respondents to bone up on the product for the study so they will sound knowledgeable.

Concern about this issue is what originally motivated me to get moderators together many years ago, a meeting that eventually led to the creation of QRCA. One week I did a focus group in New Jersey with women who were supposed to use aspirin frequently. A particularly memorable respondent was a red-haired woman wearing tinted glasses with her initial in rhinestones on one lens. The next week at the same facility, the same woman showed up for a group of *non-users*. Clearly, at least one of these times, she was lying.

Just recently, I conducted a focus group for one client at a Manhattan facility with business people on a Thursday night. The following Monday at a different facility, one of the same respondents showed up for a different business-to-business project. His demographic information was the same, which suggested he was probably telling the truth about that. When I approached him in the waiting room and said, "Weren't you in a focus group I did last week?" he first said no, then, when pressed, he "remembered." I told the clients about the situation, commenting that he had been an articulate person and asked what they wanted to do. They decided to let him participate, and he came up with a good suggestion for a product name. We reported this incident to both facilities in hopes that they would drop him out of their database. He may have been a good respondent but we don't want him showing up every week. If nothing else, "professional respondents" who go to sessions regularly can think their job is to critique product concepts and ads, rather than to express their personal feelings. The more serious problem, however, is cheating, where respondents are not who they say they are, not the people we want to interview (for example, mothers of young children or regular users of a certain brand).

A few times I've had respondents in the middle of a focus group state they've been saying they're users of the product we're discussing, but they're really not—fascinating that they would reveal this, despite the coaching. How many times does cheating occur that we don't know about? Sometimes a focus group feels fishy. Respondents who are supposedly strangers immediately are highly talkative, grabbing food across the table. Sometimes, the respondents' conversation indicates they are repeats. They

"Professional respondents" who go to sessions regularly can think their job is to critique product concepts and ads, rather than to express their personal feelings

talk about the last time they were at the facility, the fact that the refreshments are different this time, or compliment the moderator on being "better than the other ones" —a compliment we'd rather not get. Or a respondent has absolutely nothing to say about a subject, raising the question of whether he is shy or is in a group on a product he pretends to use.

Sometimes a

focus group

feels fishy

Sometimes clients assume respondents are lying. Immediately following a focus group recently, two clients rushed outside to see if any of the respondents seemed to know one another, which they consider a sign of improper recruiting. The respondents weren't talking, so they probably weren't acquaintances. The same client was convinced that several respondents in another focus group knew each other, but I didn't see any indications. Sometimes there are only a few respondents recruited two days before the group; then, suddenly, the facility announces it has filled the groups. Was this cheating? Did the facility call up the "usual suspects," as some people believe? Or did all the hard work of recruiting and leaving messages on people's answering machines finally pay off, as some field supervisors have explained to me? If cheating were really so rampant, my guess is we wouldn't have so many groups that are not filled with respondents until the very last minute. In short, no one knows for sure the extent of cheating.

While some shocking incidents are fodder for the media, most clients feel that qualitative research is of value, a sign that they believe respondents usually tell the truth. Good field services are constantly adding to their database of people interested in attending focus groups. They will then call the potential respondent and screen for a particular study. A brochure by one facility makes this statement: "To place you in the proper focus group you need to complete questions about you and your family." I once received a phone call from a well-known field service that asked for an amazing variety of information, including personal questions such as whether or not I am HIV positive or have AIDS. I was surprised, but gave answers.

One way of monitoring the repeater problem is by using a database validation service. In the U.S., Sigma is a service we use to check respondents on studies that do not entail a client list. We submit names and phone numbers in advance and the company does a "duplicate number search" to see if someone with that same name or number participated in a study in the last year and, if so, what kind (phone, mall, focus group, etc.) and what subject. In some cases, duplication is not a problem—a different person in the household was interviewed or the subject was quite different. We have, however, been able to get rid of some problem respondents, and this lets facilities know that we're watching them carefully.

Unfortunately, some facilities resist sending in names for the check, saying they are concerned about respondents being called by another service (they aren't), and a minority of moderators use Sigma. The system, too, is far from perfect. It's difficult to get complete information because people today have so many different telephone numbers. The search can help detect repeaters but not necessarily cheaters, although "professional respondents" often fall into both categories. In Canada, the Central Files database system maintained by the Professional Market Research Association has worked well in major cities. The QRCA and MRA (Marketing Research Association—a field service trade group) have a joint committee which is currently

CONTACT INFORMATION

Sigma
1275 15th Street
Suite LH
Fort Lee, NJ 07024
telephone:
201-886-0550
fax:
201-886-1413
email:
info@sigmavalidation.com

Professional Market Research Association (PMRS)
2175 Sheppard Ave. East
Suite 310
North York, Ont M2J 1WS
telephone:
416-493-4080
fax:
416-491-1670
url:
www.pmrs-aprm.com/About Us/Central.html

Marketing Research Association
1344 Sila Deane Hwy.
Suite 306
Rock Hill, CT 06067
telephone:
860-257-4008
fax:
860-257-3990
email:
email@mra-net.org

exploring database methods to weed out improperly recruited respondents in the United States.

Rescreening questionnaires also help to sort out respondents who don't belong in the groups. Often these people have just made honest mistakes in their answers. My guess is that some of the Cheaters/Deceivers may not pass the rescreen, either because they become intimidated about being caught or because they forgot what they are supposed to say. (Rescreeners are discussed in more detail later.)

Photo identification when respondents check in is now encouraged by both the QRCA and the MRA, to verify that respondents are who they say they are. Making this practice more widespread may help to scare off the professional cheaters. Alert assistants at the check-in desk will sometimes call a repeat respondent to the moderator's attention as well.

Why not use random digit dialing (RDD) out of the telephone book to find "virgin" respondents (a quaint term)? This is done on occasion, but it requires more time and money, which most clients are not willing to spend. Also, there tend to be many "no-shows"; more respondents have to be recruited, adding to higher costs.

Beyond this, moderators rely on word-of-mouth and their own instincts on which facilities they can trust. I keep my eye out for respondents I've seen before, with or without rhinestone-studded glasses.

The moderator's role in recruiting ———————

The rule for moderators is, oversee, oversee, oversee, or, in the case of some services, nudge, nudge, nudge

The rule for moderators is, oversee, oversee, oversee, or in the case of some services, nudge, nudge, nudge. Make sure that the field service has started screening when it said it would, that it has enough recruiters working on the job, and that the respondents recruited are what you asked for. We expect an update every day so we can closely monitor the process. A respondent breakdown sheet, showing all key questions for the screening and major demographics, should be filled in regularly to give us an overview of the groups. Is each group balanced the way it should be? Do all the respondents qualify? Where are the problem areas? Very simple specifications may be wrong; for a study of male golfers, the service had recruited a woman, for example.

It is to be expected that most projects will take a while to recruit, but if there are only a few respondents several days before the scheduled sessions, the study may be in trouble. We need to know if there are problems, so we can suggest possible solutions and, of course, report to our clients. Sometimes a simple change helps recruiting, like moving the time of the focus groups. At worst, we need to decide if the focus groups have to be cancelled because of recruiting difficulties.

The best field services stay in touch, tell us what problems they are encountering, and are proactive. They provide detailed summary sheets of recruited respondents for review and to pass on to our client. They make constructive suggestions on screener wording, point out unrealistic specifications, suggest a higher cooperation fee if one really seems necessary, and come up with clever ideas for recruiting low-incidence respondents. For example, to find newlyweds, look at the documents in City Hall.

Field services need to provide the moderator with complete information before a change is made in the study specifications or the cooperation fees are raised. They need to be able to answer questions like these: How many

The best field services stay in touch, tell us what problems they are encountering, and are proactive

contacts were made? How many "terminates" were there? For what reasons? The obvious solution to slow recruiting may sound like higher cooperation fees (pay people more and they'll agree to come), but a good field service will sometimes advise that money isn't the issue. Moderators need to obtain the client's approval before making such important changes.

Unfortunately, it can be enormously difficult and frustrating to obtain information on how things are going. Some facilities immediately complain that a study is hard to recruit, saying the specifications should be relaxed and the price they gave us should go up before they have spent much (or any) time recruiting. There are services that don't answer phone calls for days, don't collect the information from their recruiters, don't check to see whether their recruiters are getting the right mix for the focus groups. For example, if we asked for an even mix of employed women and homemakers, there shouldn't be nine homemakers in a group of ten. Despite our frustrations, we do go back to a few facilities because they are "the only game" in their particular town and the recruiting usually does work out in the end.

Today many projects are recruited in two weeks or less

Screening is often difficult for a variety of reasons:

The timing of the project is too short. The harder the recruit, the longer the time needed in the field. Of course, you can't start so far in advance that respondents will be reluctant to make plans. Today many projects are recruited in two weeks or less. We've had to turn down client requests for difficult-to-recruit groups within three days right before a holiday weekend. The same clients who say they want better recruiting make it nearly impossible, frankly, because of the quick turnaround.

The segment the client wants to find turns out to be a smaller than expected proportion of the population. Sometimes we know in advance that the segment will be tough to locate. Sometimes we don't. A variety of approaches can be used. For a study of women with rheumatoid arthritis, about two percent of the population, the field service contacted pharmacists, asked consumers in their database for referrals of people they knew with the condition, and placed an ad in a local newspaper to locate respondents. In some cases, though, recruiting is simply not possible or there are not enough respondents in any one market to conduct focus groups. Telephone depth interviews can be a good alternative in the latter instance.

In some cases, there are not enough respondents in any one market to conduct focus groups

The focus group is scheduled at a convenient time for the client, but respondents aren't available (clerical workers for a two-hour group at lunchtime, mothers at 3:30 when children have to be picked up at school). Changing the time of the focus group, conducting a mini-group with fewer respondents, or shortening the sessions are possible solutions.

The client's list of possible respondents, which she swore was up-to-date and accurate, has many errors. Just a few problems we have encountered: A lot of the people are dead. Some never subscribed to the magazine. Others use a different screen name when they log onto a website. Still others made a purchase after the list was compiled, or decided to be helpful and used the product before the focus group (when we wanted non-users). Sometimes the phone numbers are wrong or there are no phone numbers and many people on the list have unlisted numbers that cannot be obtained. Respondents may report different behavior than the list shows. For example, they think they are still subscribing to the magazine or they think their activity with the bank is the same vs. last year while the list says it's down a lot. It can be hard to know who's right, the respondent or the list, and a judgment has to be made about which behavior to use to assign a respondent to the proper focus group. In one memorable case, the list for an apparel designer included "Mrs. Frank Sinatra" and "Mrs. Ronald Reagan." Without some extraordinary assistance by the client, we did not think it was worthwhile contacting these potential "respondents."

Respondents on a list may also be wary. Is the study legitimate? How did the caller get their name? Often it's preferable not to tell respondents who the study's sponsor is so their answers to early questions in the sessions will be unbiased. For instance, when they are asked the name of their favorite website, they won't try to please the client by mentioning its site. Sometimes recruiting is started without revealing the sponsor and then, if results are disappointing, a client may agree to tell respondents. Other times, respondents know from the beginning. In our experience, respondents are still frank in stating their views even when they know the client's identity. We do not see any pattern of this disclosure attracting either very satisfied or dissatisfied customers.

Often it's preferable not to tell respondents who the study's sponsor is

The questions ask respondents for information they can't easily or accurately recall, so answers are likely to be different in rescreening or during the focus groups. For example, how many times did they eat a particular brand of soup six months to a year ago? Did they buy *Fitness Magazine* or a fitness magazine? Let's be honest, we don't keep such detailed records in our own minds.

The focus group categories may not fit real life. For instance, decision-makers on office equipment are not all in middle or top management, despite the stereotype. Some are office managers. A frequent problem is that the income levels clients ask for do not fit the target market. For a study of body lotions, a low-ticket item, a client may ask for women in their 20s and 30s who have $60,000+ incomes. This is an unrealistic expectation for younger or single women, because most people don't achieve that income level until they're older, especially in markets with lower incomes. In such cases, the specifications might be modified.

Questions may have different meanings to respondents than the client expected. This is especially true when vague, non-specific terms are used like "use the product regularly" or "often," and are you "aware of" a brand. Does this mean the respondent has heard of the name or really knows something about it? Is a respondent's "favorite" brand necessarily the one they "buy most often"?

Avoid vague, non-specific terms like "often," or "favorite"

Clients want respondents who have not participated often in focus groups (none in the last year, no more than three or four in total), but they are targeting a specialized group that is interviewed regularly. It is, unfortunately, difficult to keep finding dentists who haven't been in a focus group recently, since some enjoy coming and others would never consider it. At the same time, it is important to encourage the field service to go beyond its database to find "fresh" (new, not rude) respondents.

Rescreener

In addition to the initial screening, good field services rescreen at least once on the phone before the groups begin. They also confirm appointments the day of or day before the groups and send out a confirming postcard with specific directions. They stress that respondents' attendance is important and to call if there is a problem. If the respondents' agreement sounds too vague or uncommitted, they may do extra recruiting up to the time of the groups. If the weather is bad, there may be additional calls to let respondents know the groups are on.

Screening doesn't stop there. When respondents show up for the focus groups, we rescreen again just to make sure we have the right people. A written rescreener the respondent fills out is much better than having the facility host ask what are (intentionally or not) leading questions, such as, "You drink orange juice at least three times a week?" within hearing range of other respondents. Oral rescreening also presents the possibility of embarrassing respondents by asking personal questions like, "What is your household income?" in front of others.

The rescreener should be written so respondents are not led to answering in a certain way in order to qualify for the group. Wording should be the same as the original questions—a change may get different answers. To prevent respondents from feeling irritated about being asked the same questions yet again, we put in an explanation of why we do this.

Often respondents are dropped out at this stage, despite all the prior screening. In the previously mentioned case of faulty memories, we warn the clients that answers on the number of times respondents ate soup in the last year may be different. Without seeing what a package looks like, respondents may by mistake think they use another brand. They may confuse women's magazines because they seem similar. Sometimes they are conscientious and have changed their original answer, which they found was wrong. For example, they inherited more money in insurance than they first remembered. Rescreeners may sometimes catch respondents who were coached to give certain answers by unscrupulous recruiters.

Even with all this screening and rescreening, some respondents in the focus groups will contradict what they've said before. In one study, a man who was asked the "security" question said that no one in his immediate family had worked for a bank or insurance company. He said the same thing in rescreening, but immediately volunteered in the interview that his wife worked at a bank. This is maddening. However, I don't think it's necessarily a case of field services cheating, which is the conclusion clients often jump to. Rather, people don't pay close attention to questions, their memories are fuzzy, and products blur in their minds.

Sometimes what looks like a foul-up is a finding

Respondents were recruited to be viewers of a cable channel whose name is initials and whose programming format is totally different during the day and the evening. Can we really be surprised that they confused it with other cable channels that have similar-sounding acronym names? After an outburst in which he first accused the facility of coaching respondents to say they were viewers in order to fill the groups, the client learned that viewers were confused.

Sometimes the screening requirements may change during the course of a study because of what we've learned. In one project's first focus groups, for instance, we discovered that lower-income parents are not real prospects for college information sources. The beauty of qualitative research is its flexibility and the ability it provides to learn from earlier work.

Tips for field services

In addition to recruiting, field services can do a number of other things to make a project go smoothly:

Communicate with the moderator about whether or not materials needed for the sessions have arrived.

Make sure the materials are sent where they should be after the groups — to the moderator, the client, or the next facility. Often several different packages are sent out.

Provide good directions to the facility, indicating travel time from the airport and nearby hotels both at rush and non-rush hours. Getting lost or arriving late does not help the client's or moderator's mood.

Have a phone number that a live person answers during the time prior to the groups. Recently, when I called a facility from a plane that arrived three hours behind schedule in Florida to say I was on my way, I was immediately sent into voice mail hell, unable to get through. I had to call my office in New York to ask my assistant to call them — it took her three tries.

Check the audio and video equipment immediately before the focus groups. Make sure the video camera operator arrives on time and the rooms are set up the way the moderator wants them.

Have several qualitative assistants at the desk, especially in between focus groups, to check respondents in and out; an assistant to arrange and then clean the conference and back rooms, without disturbing clients listening to the sessions; and an assistant to help the moderator set up for the next group. Too often, even well-appointed facilities have one person frantically trying to do everything. Between focus groups, moderators have to speak to their clients and take care of their own needs (the bathroom is often high on the list); they shouldn't have to spend their time searching for an assistant or cleaning up.

Too often, even well-appointed facilities have one person frantically trying to do everything

Have equipment for typing concepts to be shown to respondents, computers with software programs commonly used like Microsoft Word™ and PowerPoint,™ photocopying equipment for last-minute jobs, and cooperative personnel who know how to operate the programs and equipment. On the other side, moderators and clients who show up just before the groups demanding that dozens of copies be made are unreasonable.

CHAPTER 5

Screener and Topic Guide Construction

ONCE INITIAL AGREEMENT is reached on the study objectives and desired sample, two very important documents have to be drafted:

THE SCREENER—a questionnaire the field service will use to screen or qualify respondents to participate in the project. This is needed for the recruiting process to begin. The screener is based on the client's specifications outlining what types of people should be recruited. It's important for the moderator or a client researcher familiar with the objectives of the project to write the screener. This is what usually happens, but some moderators will call in the specs and expect the field service to create a screener, a task many services are unprepared to do well.

THE TOPIC GUIDE—an outline of subjects to be covered in the actual focus group.

If it sounds easy to do these, it isn't. Translating ideas into a workable screener and guide is a challenge. Often it's not until we try to write these documents that we realize how many unanswered questions there are. Also, in the days or weeks before the sessions, clients may change their minds about what they are looking for.

An important preliminary step is to pull together information you'll need. You already have talked with the client, but clients are so close to their own products that they often lack perspective on how much "civilians" know about their product. To get the right people into the focus groups and then ask incisive questions, moderators have to see the product with fresh eyes.

Screener construction

Since qualitative research is small scale and the interviewing is conducted in the spotlight, it's important that each person is worth talking to. Writing a good screener is more of an art than a science. It's a skill that moderators are constantly working to improve.

The first step is to turn broad client specifications into concrete demographic and usage requirements. A key question to ask, especially if the client is vague, is who *don't* you want in that room? Who would be a complete waste of time to talk to?

Here is a client request we received: we want female buyers of sheets and pillowcases with incomes of $60,000+ in Cincinnati and New Jersey. Sounds straightforward, but then there are questions to ask the client:

Are there any age requirements? Does the client really want the age range to be completely open or is there a minimum (teenagers may buy sheets) or a maximum age?

How recently did they have to buy the bedding? People who bought bedding five years ago will not remember the experience.

Writing a good screener is more of an art than a science—a skill that moderators are constantly working to improve

What if the women bought other types of bedding (comforters, a set of pillowcases bought separately from sheets, dust ruffles, etc.) but not sheets? Since the study was also going to be about bedding accessories, the client might want to broaden the requirements.

Must all the respondents have incomes of at least $60,000? That's high for Cincinnati, especially for younger and single women. And since the client wanted women who shopped in discount and mass merchandisers where bedding is fairly inexpensive, this income level may be difficult to find.

In answer to the "who don't you want" question, the client said to "terminate" — which means drop out of the screening, not terminate in an Arnold Schwarzenegger way — women who only shopped at Wal-Mart or "better department stores."

Specs can be deceptively simple. Here's an example: One client said they wanted to interview magazine expires (people who did not renew their subscription). In addition to the usual demographic questions (age, income, etc.), the screener had to include questions to get at this information:

Who is the main reader of the magazine? The field service is instructed to speak with the person whose name the subscription is in, but that may not be the reader (many women, for instance, have magazines sent to their husband's name).

Did the ex-subscriber drop all or most of her subscriptions? The reasons for dropping a whole group of magazines may be very general — no time to read anything, cutting back to save money — and may not provide specific insights into the reasons for letting the client's magazine lapse.

Did the ex-subscriber receive the magazine as a gift? If the publication was not her own choice, she may never have been involved with it. (The same is true if the subscription was the publisher's substitute for a magazine that went out of business.)

Has the respondent renewed the subscription? The client's list may be out of date.

Does the person realize that her subscription has lapsed? This can't be taken for granted. Does the client want to hear from these unaware non-renewals?

Does the person read someone else's copy? If the person is reading the magazine at the office or gets it from his friend, it's probably difficult to convince him to subscribe on his own. Sometimes people let the subscription in their own names lapse because other members of the household subscribe under a special deal.

A variety of screening questions may also be needed to determine that we're talking to decision-makers. Examples include people who do all or share in the grocery shopping for the household, people who make all of their own investment decisions or share this with another person, or the person in the office who makes the purchase decisions. When the project is to study "prospects" (people whom the client thinks could become users), we'll often screen for purchasers of similar products or services. Why? The prospects for a magazine are people who already buy magazines, not people who simply read those available in doctors' waiting rooms or hair salons. And if the client's magazine is broad in scope, its subscribers are most likely not people who only read general magazines like *TV Guide* and *Reader's Digest* or a highly specific hobbyist magazine.

Some other pointers on screeners

Make the screener thorough yet concise. Respondents will simply hang up the phone if the screener takes too long, defeating the purpose of the research. Some questions can be asked in the focus group instead.

At the same time, some background information may be important. For instance, even if there isn't an income requirement, the client usually wants this demographic information for selecting the best respondents for the groups.

Construct the screener so the "terminates" come first, if at all possible. Otherwise, a respondent can go through an entire screener only to be dropped out at question 8. However, certain personal questions, like income, should not be asked too soon. It seems too abrupt to ask questions about which many people are sensitive right at the beginning.

Ask the "security" question at the beginning of the screener. The security question is intended to screen out people the client doesn't want in the groups because they (or their family members) work for the competition, or are professionals in their field atypical of regular consumers. Since most groups involve proprietary information, people who work for the media and may decide to write an article about the research also will be excluded. Some clients do not accept respondents who work in fields related to the particular study.

Our standard security question first asks, "Are you or any member of your household currently employed in any of the following occupations?" Then we ask, "Were you yourself ever employed in any of these occupations: Advertising; market research or consulting; newspaper, magazine, or broadcasting?" Fields too close for comfort for the particular study are also added. As I write this, I'm about to do some focus groups on an herbal product so the list also includes, "the manufacturing, distribution, or sales of vitamins or nutritional supplements; pharmaceutical company; nutritionist/dietitian." Sometimes it is unrealistic to be highly stringent. If you ruled out everyone in Charlotte, North Carolina, who said they or their family members or close friends ever worked at a bank, you either shouldn't be doing the groups there, or you would need to modify the security question.

Ask questions on past participation in research at the beginning of the screener as well. Some clients don't want anyone who has been in a focus group about their particular subject in the past six months or a year, or at any time. In other cases, for example, when respondents come from the client's list, this doesn't matter. If recruiting is moving slowly, clients might decide to relax this requirement.

Questions should be clear and unambiguous so respondents know exactly what you mean. Often you have to translate from the client's industry language. Don't ask which portal respondents use for the Internet. Don't ask if they buy shelf-stable foods, activity toys, or percale sheets, for example. Many people don't know or understand those terms. Wording needs to be precise. Does buying a monthly magazine "regularly" mean every month, every other month (six times a year), or what?

Make it easy for people to answer honestly and accurately. "Which, if any, of the following products do you use?" signals that it's fine to say they don't use anything on the list. "About how often would you say you do X?" lets respondents know they can make an educated guess rather than just saying they don't know. Little words and phrases make a big difference.

Disguise your interest in finding certain types of respondents. Some people may say "yes" just to qualify. If one of the first questions is, "Do you color your hair?," most people will guess that the correct answer should be yes. Instead, give respondents a list of products "some people buy" and ask which they have bought in the past year. If they mention hair color, go on to ask questions.

For many consumers, brands don't mean a whole lot. Is the cat food Friskies or Purina? The brands might all blend in consumers' minds or be differentiated only by the package color. Because memories are faulty, it may be a good idea to ask respondents to check their medicine chest or pantry to see what brand really is there. Sometimes it's useful to emphasize that we want to be sure what brand(s) respondents are buying, so they should listen carefully to the names on the list.

Being vague ("get a mix") leaves things open to misunderstanding

Spell out the instructions for the interviewer on what questions to skip (respondents who have a 401k plan get asked a certain set of questions; skip these questions for those who don't).

Specify what quotas are wanted. For example, half the respondents in each focus group should be under 50 years old, half over 50.

CLIENT LIST ISSUES

Having a customer or prospect list is essential for certain projects. Trying to find yacht owners, purchasers of a recently introduced electronic device, registered members of a website and so on can be impossible without a list from your client.

However, having a list doesn't mean that the recruiting will be easy or even, in some cases, less expensive. The list often arrives later than clients promised. Frequently there are no telephone numbers (even when the client promised them), so the field service or a computer matching service has to spend several days looking them up. That's a problem in this era of unlisted phone numbers, and it cuts into recruiting time.

Even when the client thinks a list is "clean," problems can arise. The lists can be old. People may be dead. The names might be wrong. The information may be out of date or incorrect. The people might live too far away from the facility (100 miles away, in another state). Even in the case of a good list, it may not include the information needed to find out if a respondent qualifies, so more screening will still be required. In short, thank the client for the list, but remember it's just a starting point.

Topic guide construction

The topic guide outlines the broad subject areas and, within these, questions to be covered during the focus groups. I've heard of moderators who brag that they never use a topic guide because it's inhibiting, but I think a guide serves several important purposes before and during the session:

The most

important thing

to remember

about topic

guide

construction is

that it is

intended to be

just that, a

"guide" to be

used during the

focus group, not

a "script," a term

a number of

clients use

The topic guide helps the moderator to think through the questioning process in advance. What is the client really trying to learn? What questions or research techniques may be useful?

The moderator and client can come to agreement on the interview approach. Since the "client" typically entails multiple people in a company and, in many cases, a third party (like the ad agency), everyone can be involved in reviewing the guide.

It does "guide" the moderator during the focus group, as a reminder of the approach agreed upon (at least before the first session). There are enough things to do in the group that the moderator doesn't want to worry about leaving out a key issue.

Each topic guide is custom created for a particular study. Sometimes we start from scratch. In other cases, we modify a template or old guide, adding probes tailored for the specific project. For instance, there are some probes we want to be sure to cover in exploring reactions to advertising or a new product concept.

The most important thing to remember about topic guide construction is that it is intended to be just that, a "guide" to be used during the focus group, not a "script," a term a number of clients use. Qualitative research is not a matter of mechanically going through a guide question by question without interacting with respondents. Instead, the questions are there as signposts for exploration.

Topic guides are usually developed after talking with the client. The time spent discussing the study not only is necessary for creating that piece of paper, it provides a real guideline to recognize what is important in the focus groups. I need to understand when a point brought up by a respondent hits the heart of a project's objectives, when I need to probe, and when to move on.

The questions that were answered during the initial phases of project design [see chapter 4] lay the groundwork for the topic guide. Clients new to qualitative research sometimes apologetically say, "I'm not sure how to ask this." That's fine. Clients don't need to tell me the specific questions to ask, but should communicate to me what they hope to learn. A draft topic guide sent by a client started off by asking respondents what they do about financial matters. If I were a respondent, I would have no idea of whether I was being asked to talk about bill paying, decisions on what to invest in, budgeting, or what. The question was so broad that it would have easily sent respondents off in directions irrelevant to the subject of financial planning. Interviewing the client helps to sharpen the guide. Does the client really want to know about finances in general and, if so, why?

The topic guide is a two-way conversation between moderator and client. As with the screener, the client will have a number of ideas, and the moderator also will make suggestions. I like to find out as much as I can about what the client is interested in learning, and what they want to

The time spent discussing the study not only is necessary for creating a topic guide, it provides a real guideline to recognize what is important in the focus groups

---

Issues that need to be resolved for a good topic guide include:

◼ Topics to be covered—not specific questions to be asked verbatim

◼ The general sequence of the discussion

◼ The general timing of each section

◼ Materials needed on the part of the client or the moderator

show during the groups. I also like to hear their ideas on research approaches. We can brainstorm different methods to get at the information we are seeking.

Frequently I recommend showing some materials to stimulate response after the open-ended part of the focus groups. After we have heard what respondents' perceptions of a product are, it may be useful to show the product, or in the case of food, to have respondents taste it. What are their reactions to the actual product? How do these compare to preconceptions? Ideas being considered for the future might be presented at the end of the sessions. Often I have to suggest to clients that the groups can be an opportunity to explore new directions, not just to ask about how people feel now. For a magazine, for instance, we might talk about different stories, magazine coverlines, and taglines. When special interviewing techniques seem appropriate, I might suggest a few, or we may think up something new.

Homework for writing a good guide and, of course, for effective moderating can involve studying the product, doing some observation, looking inward, and conducting some very informal pre-interviews with people I know. Familiarity with the product is crucial, yet clients often seem surprised that a researcher wants or needs to do this background work. (Just ask them what they think.")

If I'm studying a website, I have to spend time visiting the site. If I'm researching respondents' reactions to a magazine, I make sure to go through the last 12 issues of the magazine. For a study with media buyers, I review the media kit so I know how the publication presents itself to the advertising community. If I'm studying a professional association, I ask for materials like its brochure and direct-mail solicitations. If I'm studying soup, I go to the super-

After we have heard what respondents' perceptions of a product are, it may be useful to show the product, or in the case of food, to have respondents taste it

market to see where my client's product is on the shelf and how many facings (packages going across) it has compared with its competitors. If I'm doing a project for Bloomingdale's, I make the sacrifice of spending time browsing around Bloomie's. I may have to go to its competitors as well. In my case, these field trips usually benefit the stores financially.

Our role as moderators is to understand respondents' perceptions. However, simply asking people how they feel about a product isn't enough. We can better understand what's in their minds when we grasp their perspective. In the focus groups, after we have heard what respondents think, it may be necessary at times to correct their misperceptions. We're not doing this to "sell" respondents on the client's product but to probe the extent to which information can make a difference. Also, uncorrected misinformation presented by one respondent can unfairly color what others think.

Sometimes it is necessary to correct respondents' misperceptions

Even more basic, homework may be needed to understand the world you will be examining. Doing a study of diapers at the beginning of my moderator career at MPi, I was encouraged by other researchers to observe parents taking care of their infants. The fact that the entire process looked difficult and tricky helped me figure out what to ask. Self-analysis is also needed, whether the product is one I already know or have never seen before. What do I like about it, dislike, find confusing? I'm what might be called a pre-respondent before the actual research begins.

A client-prepared guide handed to the moderator may sound like a good idea, but I find it rarely is. Clients usually do this to save money, or to make interviews by different moderators on a multi-national project more consistent. Worse yet, some clients expect the moderator to go through the guide like a puppet. I recently received a topic guide that included a note that sternly instructed me not to deviate from the topic guide. "It is extremely important that you stick to the guide and make every effort to ask all of the questions in each section. Please do not embellish the material unless the guide specifically prompts you to discuss or probe further."

While a client-prepared topic guide saves me time, it doesn't save much money. It's better for the project, I believe, when I write my own. I become immersed in the project by thinking through the guide. During the groups, I have a better sense of where I'm going rather than having to reread the guide constantly. When I do work from a client guide, I still need a thorough briefing so I understand what the objective of each question is and how much depth is desired. "What kind of shopper are you?" can easily be the basis for a half-hour discussion or be just a quick ice-breaker at the beginning of the session, depending on what is needed.

"What kind of shopper are you?" can easily be the basis for a half-hour discussion

Some pointers on writing a topic guide

Think about what to ask during the respondent introductions. In addition to the respondent's name, what other information is helpful for the group and the observers to know? What will be a good opener? Clients already have a respondent spreadsheet showing a variety of product and demographic information, so there's no need to ask respondents all this. The introduction should be appropriate to the topic. I ask respondents about their households if we're talking about a consumer product. In a focus group about mothers' attitudes toward sex education for their teenage children, it obviously made sense to ask about the number and ages of all of their children, not just the teenagers. This is not necessary or appropriate for a business or professional group, of course. Asking what people do in their leisure time for fun can break the ice and give us a picture of their interests. Certain questions can quickly be asked during the introduction rather than taking time later. For a music club, for instance, ask what kind of music each respondent likes best.

Think about the session flow. The classic interview design for both qualitative and quantitative research is the inverted pyramid, going from very broad to more specific [Figure 5-1].

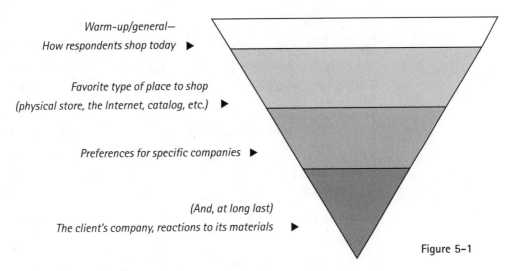

Warm-up/general—
How respondents shop today ▶

Favorite type of place to shop
(physical store, the Internet, catalog, etc.) ▶

Preferences for specific companies ▶

(And, at long last)
The client's company, reactions to its materials ▶

Figure 5-1

The pyramid approach helps to set a product in a broader context. Respondents react spontaneously before knowing, in most cases, who the client is. It's a finding when the client is mentioned unaided.

There are times when this classic flow is not appropriate or should be modified. For example, the group might start by having respondents write down the name of their favorite store. This won't be discussed until later in the group, but the answers are there on paper unbiased. In studies of advertising communication, it may be best to get a "clean" reading on the ads before respondents talk about the category as a whole.

Don't write the guide like a script — then the client won't think it is one. I want to have the freedom to vary the questions. This is not a survey! The questions I write are sometimes written as questions, sometimes as short sentences. I find a more condensed style easier to read during the focus group.

Here's a script-style topic guide a client sent me, with the instruction that questions should be read verbatim:

I would like to do a fun exercise, which asks you about the image you have of [industry type] companies. I am not looking for the products or services the company provides, but the image you think of when the company is mentioned.

■ *Many companies have an image people associate with the company. Let me give some examples. [Company X makes a game, and their image might be fun or entertaining. Company Y makes cars, and their image is sensible.]*

■ *As another example, what image do you think of when I say [Company Z]?*

■ *I am going to name several [industry type] companies and ask a few questions related to the company's image.*

[For each of the six companies listed below, ask questions A–D]

■ *a) What image comes to mind when you think of [company name]? I am not looking for the product the company makes, but the image you think of when the company is mentioned. It can be anything at all that you associate with the company, a symbol, a picture, a person, a feeling.*

■ *b) What words describe your image [company name]?*

■ *c) How would you describe [company name] to someone who is not familiar with [company name]?*

■ *d) What does [company name] stand for?*

The questions here are fine, but so highly detailed that a moderator could come across as stiff reading each one word for word with her head down. Respondents may answer the basic question about a company image without being asked points a-d in strict order. Doing this would be extremely tedious for respondents and probably more time-consuming than the client really wants. Even with such a detailed script, the moderator still needs to think spontaneously of alternative wording when, as happened in one session, respondents had trouble understanding the image concept.

Here's the condensed style version I prefer. This approach is far easier for me to follow and has the advantage of observers being less literal in expecting me to read the questions aloud as they appear on the page.

Think of company images beyond their actual products or services. Example: [Company X's product] is [game name], the image is fun/entertaining. [Company Y's product] is a car. Its image is sensible. What is [Company Z's] image?

Image of [industry type] companies. (*As needed, probe:*) any associations (words, symbol, mental picture, person/type of person, feeling, what it stands for).

I don't write "why" after each question but, since clients who don't know me sometimes get nervous, I often send a

"As needed, probe:" *is useful as a prompt in moderating and to signal observers that the probe will not be asked if respondents have already answered the question*

note explaining that I will probe. When I started doing focus groups, I wrote 20-page topic guides with probes for every possible respondent answer I could think of. These were impossible to follow, so the topic guides I write now are considerably shorter (3 to 5 pages).

Consider written exercises at one or two points in the discussion; don't overburden the group with writing because it can get boring. Having respondents write down their feelings can help to avoid group bias—and avoid your client thinking that group bias has occurred. This is especially helpful when respondents are looking at materials they have never seen before. In the bedding study we recently completed, respondents "shopped" in silence right after the introductions, then wrote down which of the samples shown they would and would not consider buying. When virtually all wrote they would not think of the new fabric the company was planning to market, no one on the client side could think a few negative respondents had influenced reactions. At the same time, respondents who liked the fabric had committed themselves on paper and did speak up.

Writing down free associations on a topic can also provide insights into individual feelings while bringing up issues for the group to discuss together.

Think about the order of showing materials. Materials are often presented one at a time: concept 1 is discussed, then concept 2, and so on until the end. The sequence will be rotated in later groups to avoid order bias. In my experience, order bias can help *or* hurt the first materials. Sometimes the first one seen is considered the most exciting. When respondents become "educated" by seeing a series of concepts for a product they don't know

Having respondents write down their feelings can help to avoid group bias—and avoid your client thinking that group bias has occurred

about, they may like the one at the end. There's another issue, though — fatigue. Respondents may not like the last concept simply because they're worn out.

In some cases, it may be best to lay out all the materials at the same time. Respondents are asked to write down which they prefer, perhaps ranking their top favorites, and to indicate if there are any they reject. This approach deals with both order and group bias. An online company was looking at about a dozen alternative "creative architectures," one-paragraph ideas for advertising strategy written in a fairly straightforward manner. These were typed on two pieces of paper; half of each group saw one page first, half the other page first. The discussion then focused on the concepts which respondents said would be most likely to interest them in the website. After these ideas were probed thoroughly, respondents were asked if any of the other ideas had elements of appeal to them.

Order bias can help or hurt the first materials

Consider projective questions, especially for imagery. Indirect questions and exercises [see Chapter 9] can be great ways to "get below the surface" of respondents' rational comments. I sometimes put these in the guide as "optional," deciding during the session if the direct discussion has given us what we need, or if further work is needed.

Keep in mind that the timing of the sections can, at best, be approximate for the first group. After that, we can plan more realistically. The big unknown, of course, is whether respondents will have a lot or a little of interest to say on a subject. In a recent study of a professional association, when non-contributors knew nothing beyond its name, the other questions in the outline became irrelevant.

Like a screener, the topic guide may also go through several drafts as the clients give it more thought. I may have further ideas as well. I like to meet with the client for a last-minute review an hour before the first group: What does the client consider to be the key questions, what questions are optional or can be asked briefly? Sometimes I'll realize I'd like to change a question right before the group is about to start.

The best groups are conversational, following the flow of respondents' comments

The guide continues to evolve during the focus group process. Our first guide is just our educated guess on the best way to approach the first focus group. Flexibility is essential. In writing a guide, I'm often aware that the sequence of some questions is arbitrary. I put them in what seems to be a reasonable order, but the best groups are conversational, following the flow of respondents' comments, not rigidly marching from question 3 to question 4 to question 5 for no reason other than that's the way they appear on paper. On a few occasions, I have had clients ask why I went out of order.

During the first session, I'll often scribble notes on additional questions that may be good to ask in subsequent sessions and other questions the client asks during or after the group. We can't necessarily anticipate whether respondents will have a lot or almost nothing to say on a subject. Since focus groups are intentionally interactive and serendipitous, we can't know what interesting areas will emerge that need to be probed. Topic guides are dynamic documents. After the initial group or day of interviewing, the guide can change so dramatically that I often hand write a new condensed version for myself [see Figure 5-2]. Flexibility is key. The guide can be dramatically modified or even totally rewritten in between groups. In a recent 12-group study, the client gave me direction on what special

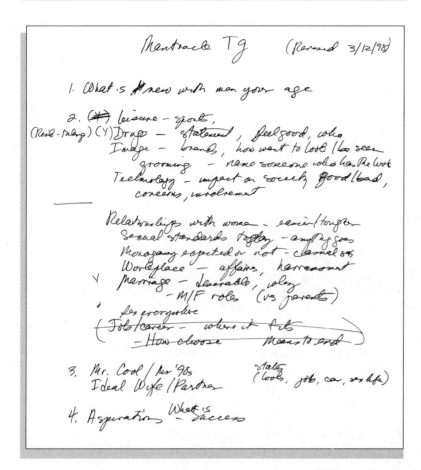

Figure 5–2

points to probe for each session. For the last session, he said that the lifestyle segment, about half an hour in the other groups, could take the full two hours. I usually don't append a topic guide to a report since the original one can be so different from the final one. The methodology section outlines the general question areas, which I consider sufficient as a record.

CHAPTER 6

Moderating: The Listening Loop

A moderator must know the business issues of the research. I think that the biggest differences among moderators is how well they probe. Some moderators are frenetic, others just sit back and wait for responses to happen. Personally, I like a more aggressive moderator. I've worked with moderators who are so laid back that I got nervous we would never get to the answer.
—*Mike Schwartz,* Campbell Soup Company

The choice of a moderator is very subjective. Some want a moderator who's very strong in the focus group room and probes everything right then. Other moderators probe later. Other moderators are more like a psychiatrist, and just let the participants talk, coming back at the end of a particular section to probe. They are more loose—some clients love that, some don't. It depends on how comfortable you are with ambiguity. Some clients are more trusting as opposed to wanting a moderator who follows the guide. I feel **you can get to the same place, whatever the style.**
—*Linda Thorp,* Marketing Research, American Express

You have to have a high level moderator who has a knowledge of your product and has good interviewing techniques. **The moderator also has to have a comfort level with your product or your industry.** I would never hire someone who doesn't know *The New York Times.*
—*Wendy Robinson, The New York Times*

A good moderator listens and builds on the topic guide. A few days ago, we did groups where the moderator didn't take the initiative to probe and didn't look for synergies. Some moderators just go down their checklist and stick to the guide, but you have to be much more analytical and ready to probe.
—*Andy Semons,* Ogilvy & Mather

THIS IS WHERE IT ALL HAPPENS. The focus group is what we've been planning, and what we'll analyze afterwards. The importance of this phase and the fact that this is when clients usually watch is the reason why qualitative researchers are called moderators, whether they like it or not.

The respondents are assembled, presumably meeting all the client's specifications. The clients are seated behind the one-way mirror awaiting enlightenment, sometimes fearing a bashing. Now it's up to the moderator to go after the information needed in the two hours, typically attempting to cover a jam-packed topic guide.

For better or worse, there is a theater aspect to a focus group conducted in front of the one-way mirror. Observers are unobserved themselves, watching strangers interact. The moderator is highly aware of having two audiences to keep involved and pleased. One of the charges made against focus groups is that they are "entertainment" for the back room. Clients may judge the quality of the group and the moderator by the liveliness of the session, for instance, rather than the productiveness of the process. A focus group that seems slow and boring to the observers may reveal very useful information but, without the "bells and whistles," the groups may not be considered effective by clients. Sometimes it's necessary to explain to the observers that the group they just saw was unexciting but very useful.

A focus group that seems slow and boring to the observers may reveal very useful information

Two great ways to learn about facilitation are to be a respondent (to observe other moderators) and to participate in groups yourself.

Starting out watching other people moderate gave me ideas about what to do—and what not to do. My positive moderator role models made respondents feel comfortable and were highly creative in pursuing issues that offered insights. However, there were also negative models. One man started a group by announcing to the group of home-makers that he was in charge. Just the fact that he was sit-ting in the head chair and asking the questions established his authority without have to make this off-putting decla-ration. Another used four-letter words at the beginning of a focus group with middle-aged respondents.

On the participation side, I've been a respondent at a QRCA session and in a study another research organization held about its conferences. Of course, these weren't typical focus groups and I wasn't a typical respondent. I knew other respondents, had very strong feelings and a professional connection to the topics being dis-cussed. Both sessions demonstrated to me just how effective the focus group process can be. As we talked, more thoughts came to mind, things I might not have remembered to mention if I had been inter-viewed individually. The group's ideas built on other ideas. By the end, I think our suggestions were richer because of the interaction.

GOOD RESPONDENT ETIQUETTE

▶ *Don't interrupt*

▶ *Don't answer too often*

▶ *Don't talk to neighbors*

▶ *Don't play assistant moderator, probing other respondents' answers*

In the conference study, it was terrific to be able, finally, to tell the organization what I really thought and to feel my comments might have an impact. Even though I knew the higher-ups were observing so they would know I was crit-ical, I was focused on speaking my mind. "Group bias" is one of the most commonly criticized aspects of focus groups, but it didn't seem to be a problem either time. Everyone seemed to stay true to his or her own opinions while being open to hearing the points of view of others.

During the sessions, my attention was centered solely on the other people in the room. Knowing what "good respondent" etiquette is, I tried, sometimes struggled, to follow it — not to interrupt, not to answer too often, not to talk to my neighbor and, most of all, not to play assistant moderator, probing other respondents' answers. Especially difficult was being told to move on when I was eager to say something.

Moderator styles

I once conducted a focus group on a well-known prescription product that was not identified by name. The respondents repeatedly brought up safety concerns, and I told them that the product was approved by the FDA, but they weren't convinced. The client told me to "knock it on its head" immediately if the respondents asked about safety, forcefully cutting them off. She was right that we did need to move on, and the discussion of safety wasn't helpful after a point, but how do you get the group to move on without quashing respondents? That's a question of moderating style.

On one extreme, there's the *passive moderator style*, where the moderator asks questions from the guide, but doesn't intervene in the process to either keep the group on course or bring up new ideas. A good moderator, according to some people, is the one who does very little talking.

On the other extreme, there is the *aggressive moderator style*. Here, the moderator is highly dynamic, clearly the authority figure and the star of the show. There's the flamboyant moderator, who even jumps up on the table to get attention (yes, this is a real person). Some clients like it; it's colorful. There's also the confrontational moderator who tells respondents, "You're lying" or "You're full of it" (sometimes specifying what the "it" is).

The passive moderator style asks questions from the guide, but doesn't intervene in the process

ACTIVE MODERATOR

▶ *Pursues new directions*

▶ *Explores new ideas*

▶ *Gives respondents needed information*

I believe in the middle ground, the *active moderator style.* The moderator does far more than just ask the questions in the topic guide, keep the conversation on track, and attempt to get all the respondents to participate. The active moderator probes in deeper and more creative ways. This includes pursuing new directions, exploring new ideas, and giving respondents information when it is needed. Why have respondents spend half an hour talking about the product based on incorrect facts? At times, I may prod respondents to tell me more, while maintaining my neutrality. Sometimes it's important to emphasize to the group that I'm just trying to understand, not to sell them on anything. Depending on the personalities in a particular group, I may say a lot or relatively little.

If respondents seem to me to be rationalizing or are not forthcoming, I may challenge them, but I don't believe in calling someone a liar. Moreover, I don't believe in embarrassing people. For instance, in a study of romance novels, a client wanted me to ask the female respondents how often they had sex. I refused.

There are gentler ways of getting the truth. Respondents have agreed to come in and help us out; they are being paid, but they are still doing us a favor. They want to feel that they have had a chance to express their feelings and that they got something from hearing the comments of other people, and most of all, that they were valued and respected. If the experience is unpleasant, they will not return in the future and they will tell others not to participate. A client who was a focus group respondent one time said he had been frustrated that there was no chance to express his feelings; he was not treated badly but got nothing out of being there. Treating respondents well helps the research industry as whole.

The job of being a good moderator starts with dressing to play the part. Appearance is one element of establishing rapport with respondents. Moderators don't have to look just like the respondents they are interviewing, but they do have to be unintimidating, not too remote. I give a lot of thought to what I wear for each type of session, dressing at or close to respondents' level of formality and sophistication, yet clearly in my role as moderator.

The job of being a good moderator starts with dressing to play the part

If it's an executive group, at least some respondents, even in these casual times, will probably be wearing business attire. A few years ago, women all wore dresses or suits with silk blouses, but now it's often pants suits with a turtleneck, so that's how I dress, too. For an upscale group, I dress up a little, although still in a casual way. For a downscale group, I dress more informally, less expensively. For a fashionable group, it's more up-to-date (you can never go wrong in all black). For a mainstream group in a conservative area, nothing high fashion or offbeat. For a teenage group, neat casual (no suits) that is somewhat hip without trying too hard, but not jeans, because that looks like you're not serious about your job. Other no-nos are funky eyeglasses, large eye-catching jewelry, and seductive necklines. All these are distracting and unprofessional looking. A toy company that conducted focus groups with children told me that they asked another moderator to undo her bun and remove her glasses (she wasn't very nearsighted) to soften her severe teacher look.

At times, I feel I look more boring than the way I normally dress, and I'm sometimes concerned that my clients will think I'm a boring person as a result, especially the highly sophisticated ones. My goal, though, is to dress for the front room, not for the back room.

Making the group work

Qualitative research is an opportunity to find out more about what people mean, to probe apparent contradictions, to get beneath the surface

What's going through the moderator's mind during the focus group? Good moderators are not just question machines; they're investigators, detectives striving to learn. Particularly with the growth of online research, there's a misconception that all open-ended questions are qualitative research. That's not true. Asking, "How would you rate this website?" is just a starting point. What does a rating of 5 or 8 mean; why did the respondent give a high or a fairly low rating? The value of qualitative research is the opportunity to find out more about what people mean, to probe apparent contradictions, to pursue new lines of questions, to find out the reasons behind their statements and actions, to get beneath the surface of facile responses. If a respondent answers a question and it doesn't make sense, it's the moderator's job to understand why.

Getting the group started: moderator introduction

Moderators pay a great deal of attention to their introductions. A highly respected moderator once told the QRCA that she continually practices her introduction. This part of the session, in fact, contains several debated elements.

Some introductions are long, detailing the ground rules and telling respondents what the people behind the mirror are doing. One moderator whose tape I was asked to review gave a ten-minute spiel which included the fact that the clients were eating their sandwiches but left out the nicety of telling respondents her name.

Here's the introduction I use, with some modifications:

As you're getting settled, let me first thank you for coming tonight and giving us your time [especially at rush hour/in bad weather]. I'm Judy Langer. As you probably know, we're doing a study about X [whatever subject is in the screener]. We like to make things informal, so please feel free to help yourself to refreshments whenever you want. We'd like to hear from all of you on your feelings. [If it's technical subject with consumers: I'm not an expert and I don't expect you to be one either. Whether you feel you know a little or a lot about the subject, that's very helpful to us.] Please feel free to come into the conversation at any time. If somebody says something, I always like to know how other people around the table feel. Sometimes people agree and other times people have different views. You don't have to wait for me to ask you a question. If we need to move along in the interest of time, I'll let you know. Just so you know, we audiotape [and videotape] so we can go back and review the tapes, so please talk one at a time so I can hear you when I listen to the tapes later. [If ads, new-product concepts, or other materials will be shown: Later on, I'll be showing you some things we want to get your reactions to; I'm not personally involved in any of it, so whatever you think is what I need to hear.]

This introduction tells respondents several things:

- Their time is appreciated.
- They should feel at home, while still recognizing that the group has a purpose.
- Their thoughts and feelings are wanted.
- Active participation is desired and expected.

■ They should not feel embarrassed or hesitant to speak up if they aren't especially knowledgeable.

■ They can feel free to speak at any time.

■ At the same time, they are given notice that the moderator may have to cut them short for research reasons.

■ The ground rule of speaking one at a time and why it matters.

■ The group is being observed and taped—this is done for legal reasons and simply because it's the right thing to do.

■ The moderator is neutral/objective—they don't have to worry about their comments pleasing or hurting my feelings.

I say this introduction in a tone that (I hope) communicates that the research will be interesting for the respondents. It's important right in the beginning to encourage respondents to feel free to say what's on their minds and to realize that each one is expected to participate. They also need to know that we're not looking for consensus as many meetings are.

Here are some of the items in the intros used by some other moderators that I purposely leave out, and why:

"Feel free to comment, whether it's negative or positive, about any of the things we will be discussing today." It's better to avoid the word "negative," which may suggest respondents are encouraged to be critical some of time.

"I have nothing to sell you." This is stated in the screening, and we can assume respondents who have agreed to come already accept that this is legitimate research.

"Please speak as loudly as I do." It sounds preachy. Respondents pay no attention to this instruction anyway.

"You are being paid to have courage and speak up." This suggests that respondents will be asked to risk disapproval, which may put them on guard. Up to now, they may not have given any thought to possible embarrassment.

"You do not need to answer every question." Why make a point of telling respondents they don't need to participate at times since they usually don't try to anyway?

"Avoid side conversations with the person next to you." Telling respondents you want them to speak one at a time (along with the reason why) suffices and is said in a more positive way.

"There are no right or wrong answers." My first reaction when I hear something like this is, "Yeah, right." It's also condescending. That's not really true if we ask questions of fact/knowledge.

"We may bring up subjects that may be a little embarrassing to talk about in front of strangers. Your candor will help many others in your situation." This seems heavy-handed, calling attention to potential discomfort if the topic is a sensitive subject. I'd prefer not to say anything at the beginning, moving into the subject when respondents seem at ease. Alternatively, there are ways of dispelling awkwardness. In a hemorrhoid study, I started by saying, "I realize this is not a subject you usually sit around a table talking about, but everyone here has the same problem." Respondents laughed and inevitably one said that hemorrhoids are "a pain in the butt," then proceeded to talk freely about the problem.

"Please show respect for others' comments and don't make fun of anyone." It's very rare that a respondent mocks another one. If it happens, the moderator can take care of it on the spot. Why assume that people won't treat others with respect? It's like saying to a guest, "Welcome to my house. Please don't put your feet on my furniture, kick my cat, or leave a mess behind." Respondents might also feel they are being told to hold back comments if they disagree with each other.

Long-winded introductions may create the impression that the research will be like school or a formal meeting, rather than an opportunity to express one's views and feelings, which most people enjoy doing

Delivered in the right tone of voice, these introductory remarks might work. However, I'm concerned that they could set a tone of lecturing, and that they plant negative suggestions that respondents have to be somewhat wary and on guard. Long-winded introductions may also create the impression that the research will be like school or a formal meeting, rather than an opportunity to express one's views and feelings, which most people enjoy doing.

Personal information about the moderator should be left out unless it helps to elicit information for the study. We're there as neutral people with whom respondents can feel free to share their feelings. They don't need to know if we're single or married, what city we're from, our hobbies, and so on. Why purposely make it clear that you're different from the respondents? Even in the South, respondents may not think my Yankee accent means I'm from up North since there are so many transplants these days. If they ask where I'm from, I'll usually say, "I'll tell you at the end." I avoid letting them know I'm from New York, a city that frequently inspires negative feelings. On the other side, when I do focus groups with parents about their children I will often say, "I don't have kids so you'll have to tell me about it."

Getting the group started: respondent introduction

Some moderators dispense with the respondent introduction, and a few clients have suggested I save time this way. I strongly believe some kind of respondent introduction, however short, is essential. Respondents feel they have been recognized as individuals and that they have some idea of who all these other people are. Many of the same customs that make people comfortable in your home apply to creating the right atmosphere in a focus group.

While I typically say, "Tell us your name, first name is fine," most respondents do give their full names. The information we ask for in going around the table is relevant to the discussion, even if it's not apparent from the outset. Respondents will often refer back both to their own and other people's information during the discussion—"Well, you're single, so maybe it's different for you."

Sometimes there's a sense of awkwardness in providing this information at the start but, almost invariably, either a respondent or I will make a joke that serves as an ice-breaker. A respondent says, "I've been married for 30 years —to the same man!" or after a respondent mentions having children aged 25, 20, and 2, I'll just say, "Wow!"

It's fascinating what people choose to reveal in their intros. When I did a demonstration focus group for a professional association, one man stated that he is gay and lives with his lover, a fact other members of the organization who had worked with him for decades did not know. This is the time when I may volunteer some relatively unimportant piece of personal information if it makes a respondent more comfortable. Singles in a room full of married people often say, "I guess I'm the only one here," so it helps if I say, "Me too." If a respondent says he or she

Respondents will often refer back both to their own and other people's information during the discussion

loves ballroom dancing and this is completely irrelevant to the subject, I may say I do as well. Dancing is reliably uncontroversial.

Some respondent intros for consumer groups

"Please tell us your name, your occupation [or] what you're doing these days; if you're a full-time homemaker or work outside the home or in a business." This shows respect for homemakers as having an occupation. "Tell us what your household is like, if you're married or single, live with other people, if you have kids at home, how old they are, and some of the things you like to do for fun." If we ask what people do in their spare time, they say they don't have any spare time. Some moderators disapprove of asking occupation because it establishes hierarchy in the sessions. White-collar workers are typically more comfortable with this than blue-collar workers, but respondents usually realize this is important information.

Some moderators disapprove of asking occupation because it establishes hierarchy in the sessions

Some straightforward questions might be added here rather than asked in the warm-up, saving time and giving us a picture of each respondent. For an arthritis study, for instance, "Briefly [key word] tell us about when your arthritis was diagnosed and what your symptoms are." Sometimes I'll add, "not your whole life story," letting respondents know, nicely, that they should not be long-winded.

A business intro after asking for the respondent name:

"Please tell us what company or organization you work for. If it's a name we might not recognize, what industry or field it is in, what your job and responsibilities are."

A simple variation on "Introduce yourself" is "Introduce the person next to you." This works especially well with teenagers. They are given a few minutes to talk with their neighbor to find out information like "Where they go to school, what they like to do, if they have any brothers and sisters." Some of this information is helpful for other respondents, the observers, and me to know—some of it is just a way to get teens talking.

Here's what I don't ask: respondents' age. Some moderators contend that this is a great icebreaker, immediately communicating to the group that they are being asked to be honest. Most respondents, they insist, tell their ages (or an age, at any rate). Those who refuse to tell or are vague ("25+") reveal their reluctance to be open. This question seems to me both unnecessary and uncomfortable. Typically, the moderator and client already know the age, or at least an age range, for each respondent, so why ask people to state this right at the beginning? People can more or less guess one another's age within a few years anyway. Asking respondents how old they are implies that this is important in the conversation and the way they will be seen. It's not only "older" people who might be made uncomfortable either; young people may feel judged by their lack of experience. Think about the "real world"—people are not usually asked their age in business or social settings, while "what do you do?" is common.

Asking respondents how old they are implies that this is important

The warm-up section

The first part of the discussion is usually a "warm-up," intended, as the name suggests, to make respondents comfortable with the focus group process and open to the questions that will follow. Some moderators ask a series of questions unrelated to the project just as an icebreaker, then tell respondents they are moving into the real subject of the research, but why waste valuable time going nowhere? The warm-up should be useful in itself, not a throwaway. A technique of another moderator, which I heard about from an impressed client, is to tell the group that one of the respondents has not shown up. Pointing to an empty seat, the moderator asks the group to imagine what George is like —what does he look like, what kind of job does he have, etc. Then the moderator reveals that there is no George but that the respondents have done a wonderful job of using their imaginations and that this is what is wanted from them in the research. This approach is too cute and manipulative for my taste.

Good moderating

should look easy

Warm-up questions, however brief, should:

Be an easy attitude question everyone has some feelings about, and should be open ended, not a cut-and-dried behavior question. A free association question like, "What comes to mind when you think of cats?" is a lot better than, "Do you serve dry or wet cat food?"

Involve each respondent in the focus group. While clients are often impatient to "get on with it," it's essential that every respondent be given a chance to talk or, if they don't volunteer, be invited in. This sets the tone for the rest of the session, making it clear that all should take an active role.

Make clear that respondents will be expected to think, not just give pat answers. Asked their feelings about convenience stores, respondents will often say, "They're convenient," which gets us nowhere. Follow-up probes on how and when they're convenient and why respondents choose to go there rather than another type of store lead us to useful information. This is when respondents talk about the supposedly "non-rational" factors that matter. For instance, they may say that they have a favorite store where they feel at home.

The moderator's mind

Good moderating should look easy. The moderator should appear comfortable — engaged with respondents and the process. In reality, moderating is very challenging, with the moderator's mind working on many different levels simultaneously. There are several aspects to the moderator's role:

Interviewer — asking not only the questions written in the topic guide but knowing when to follow up, when to go in new directions suggested by an unexpected answer, thinking of what to ask in order to better understand.

Manager of group dynamics — establishing and maintaining a productive group process among respondents, dealing with problems that arise.

Research analyst — developing hypotheses that might solve the client's marketing, advertising, and other problems; exploring these in the sessions.

Research supplier — keeping the client satisfied that the company's objectives are being met.

> THE MODERATOR MUST KEEP IN MIND THREE DIFFERENT TIME FRAMES:
>
> ▶ PAST: *What has been said*
> ▶ PRESENT: *What is being said*
> ▶ FUTURE: *What is the next question/topic*

And the moderator's mind is focusing on different time frames:

Past: what respondents have already said, what has already been covered.

Present: what respondents are saying now, asking the right questions at the right time, figuring out what it means.

Future: where the discussion is and should be going.

Moderators need to have a balance of discipline and creativity. They need to follow the flow of conversation while staying on topic. They need to keep to the schedule—paying attention to the rough time estimates for different parts of the topic guide, keeping their promise to let respondents leave on time—yet be loose enough to pursue important issues that arise.

I think of moderating as a "listening loop"—processing all kinds of information while you're hearing it and deciding immediately what to do with it. The moderator is not just a question machine, throwing out questions to the group, asking the standard and obvious probes ("Tell me more." "What does that mean to you?").

Qualitative research should be a truly interactive, dynamic process, not a static one

Qualitative research should be a truly interactive, dynamic process, not a static one. The difference between qualitative and quantitative research is not just that we ask open-ended questions. The real difference is that qualitative research is truly open to hearing what respondents have to say. If they don't understand a question, we reword it. If they don't answer a question directly, we ask it again or find another way to ask it. If they say something that's vague, we dig for more information. If they say something that conflicts with the client's hypotheses, we try to find out more. If they say something unexpected that might suggest ideas on how the client can solve a problem, we also probe more deeply. If we're looking for great quotes and a respondent says something colorful, we ask for more.

While clients often call a topic guide a "script," a good moderator uses this as a starting point of subjects to be covered, not necessarily in that order. One of the biggest complaints clients make about moderators is that many are "wooden," strictly following that "script" no matter what comes up. It's easier to ask canned questions in pre-written order than it is to think every minute about whether you're learning all you need to.

Clients are at least partially responsible for the problem in their quest for constantly "new," "cutting edge," and even "fun" techniques. Clients may tell the moderator about some great question they heard in another focus group and want asked on a completely different project. Some examples: Have respondents close their eyes and imagine the product as a room, ask them what kind of song the product would be, write the brand's obituary, do a collage of the brand but take only a few minutes, and so on.

TIP: MAKE THE MOST OF THE GROUP'S ENERGY

I believe strongly in a serendipitous style of interviewing, an invisible technique that follows the flow and uses the energy of the group. There are wonderful moments when a respondent opens up or when the group gets excited about something. Unless there's a very good reason to delay asking a question that appears later in the topic guide (for instance, you don't want to ask too much about one particular store in the introductory phase), why not ask it now? Once the energy of the group is diffused, it may be difficult to get it going again. When a valuable comment is made, this is the time to ask for more information, to dig deeper. This also makes respondents feel they are heard and understood.

Moderator's internal Q&A _____

Here are just some of the questions moderators should constantly be asking themselves during the interviewing process.

What else do I need to ask to understand this respondent's statement — what did she mean, why does she feel that way? Approaches include obvious probes like, "Tell me more," "What do you have in mind?" "Please explain that." You can also refer back to an earlier comment and ask if respondents' feelings have anything to do with the childhood experiences they mentioned.

The moderator has to keep track mentally of who has spoken and who has been left out

Is there anyone I've left out that I need to get to? There is no need to ask every respondent every question—this could easily turn into tedious and undynamic serial one-on-ones, another major complaint I hear from clients about moderators. On key questions, though, I do try to get to everyone. This shows respect for respondents. It's important to keep track mentally of who has or hasn't talked yet. If you forget, as I sometimes do, it's okay occasionally to ask the group, "Who didn't I get to?"

What did this respondent say earlier? If the pieces don't fit, I need to find out why. It's also a way to show people that you've been listening. Approaches: Ask the respondent to explain the contradiction without implying that the respondent is foolish or lying. You might say, "I remember you said that you have more free time now, but you also said you don't have time to go to the dentist. Tell me about that."

Am I hearing everything I need to know to understand the problem and answer the objectives of the research? Is there a question that's not in the topic guide that I should ask? Does what respondents are saying make sense to me or not? Do I feel I understand why they feel, believe or do what they do—and, if I don't, what part of the puzzle is missing?

What did respondents not say that we expected to hear or that seems conspicuously absent? What did respondents in the earlier groups say that didn't come up here? If there's a discussion of brand choice, for instance, and price is never mentioned, the moderator needs to ask about its role.

Do respondents seem to be agreeing with one another genuinely or has "group think" settled in? Approaches to get beyond group bias: Have respondents write down their reactions independently, which forces them to think through their feelings and "commit" to them. Break the group into teams with loud mouths in separate subgroups. Tell the group, "A respondent in another group said . . ." to give quiet respondents an opportunity to express a different view.

Are respondents telling me what they really think or are they being socially or politically correct? This is an area of great debate among clients. It can be very hard to tell. To find out, you could just ask: "Really? Why is that a problem? Do you think other people feel that way?"(See next two questions).

What does respondents' body language tell me beyond their words? Cues: leaning into the table = interest; leaning away = lack of interest or boredom; eyes opened wider, making eye contact with the moderator = desire to talk (call on that respondent); yawn = boredom or stuffy air; rolling eyes = disagreement/skepticism; putting the hand on the heart = deep feelings; crossed arms = lack of involvement, possible disagreement. Understanding this body language is important in itself and can stimulate ideas for follow-up questions, especially when gestures and expressions conflict with words.

What does the tone of voice of the individual respondents and of the group as a whole tell me? Here you look for changes in loudness and pace. Cues: flat tone of voice = saying what the respondent feels they are supposed to say without strong convictions; suddenly speaking loudly and excitedly = intense feelings (tone can indicate enthusiasm, annoyance, etc.); giggling = discomfort; hushed tone = seriousness, sadness. Sometimes there's a big energy whoosh in the group—everyone becomes highly animated in a happy or angry way, or laughter erupts.

What am I hearing that surprises me or that conflicts with what the client expected? It's important to follow it up and find out if other respondents in that and subsequent groups feel that same way.

Do I have a clear picture of what this product or service is really doing for people, or are they just stating the obvious? Are they playing back product attributes, or are they telling me about benefits? If they keep focusing on features, how do I probe to find out more? Approaches: You might say, "You mentioned that this magazine makes you feel better informed. Tell us why that matters to you." "What does it mean for you that the product has this ingredient?" "Can you think of a time when it really helped you?"

How much time do I have left? Will I be able to cover everything when just one section of the topic guide could take the full two hours? Approaches: Keep an eye on the clock without being too strict. Don't dwell on something that's interesting to you but may not be to the client. If necessary, check in the back room with the client to let them know the group is going long and they'll have to choose what to cover and what to skip. Some moderators let the focus group run over for 15 or 30 minutes without asking respondents' permission, but it's not a good idea. Respondents become restless. Some need to get home, and it's unfair since they've contracted for a certain amount of time. In a few instances when there's been a tremendous amount to cover, I've asked respondents if they would stay for extra money. One respondent happily answered she would stay for the entire weekend if the price was right.

What does all this mean anyway? What am I learning about consumers' feelings, beliefs, and behavior? What ideas does this suggest about solving the particular marketing problem? The analysis does not start after the groups are completed. As we develop hypotheses, we explore them in the focus group we're conducting or in the ones to follow. Approaches: Ask yourself if you feel you understand respondents' motivations, the product's tone and benefits. Think about how a client might use the information.

Dealing with challenges

Beyond keeping the group on schedule and in focus, the moderator also faces other challenges. Here are some suggestions for dealing with common situations.

How can I get a dominating or digressing respondent to stop talking without embarrassing him, while maintaining warm rapport both with that person and the group as a whole?

Approaches: Circling the room helps here, with the problem respondent going last. There are a variety of nice-
but-firm (NBF) ways of getting that person to tone down
(more about this later).

**How can I get the quiet members of the group to feel comfort-
able and accepted enough to participate easily?** It's fascinating that a shy respondent who hasn't volunteered will
sometimes suddenly blossom when asked for his opinion, becoming an active participant for the rest of the session. On the other side, there are people who remain
bashful or merely parrot what previous respondents have
said. Benign neglect can be the best policy. Clients often
judge moderators by their skill in getting all the respondents to speak about equal amounts but, despite our best
efforts, this may not be possible or even desirable. (For
more approaches see pp. 137–139)

**When I have a "know-it-all" respondent who is critical of the
others or of the client, how do I prevent this person from
spoiling the free-flowing atmosphere?** Approaches: make it
clear that the discussion will first cover positives and then
turn to negatives (the message is, everything will be
heard, you just have to wait); directly tell the know-it-
all, "I'm going to save you for last since you're an expert
on this subject." In a focus group on a website, one man
quickly spieled off a bunch of Internet acronyms. Silence
descended on the group and the less Internet-savvy
respondents looked slightly dazed. "I have absolutely no
idea what you're talking about," I said in a humorous
way, signaling that it was okay for the other respondents
to be ignorant and that this guy didn't need to try to
impress us, without embarrassing him. In another study,
when it became clear that one man would make only

curt, sarcastic, and unhelpful remarks about the client, enjoying disagreeing with the other respondents, I chose not to call on him for the rest of the group. He did not signal any interest in speaking, so this worked out well.

If the entire focus group has become highly negative toward the client's product, how do I keep the research open and objective without making respondents feel manipulated or suppressed? When a focus group becomes highly critical in tone, respondents are sometimes embarrassed to admit they have positive feelings. We certainly need to hear criticisms of the client's product, even if the client doesn't enjoy the experience, but it is important to avoid letting the focus group turn into bashing for the sake of bashing. Approaches: "Now that I know what you don't like about the product, I need to hear what it has going for it." Or, "Let's brainstorm constructive suggestions on ways of improving the product."

If the concept is getting a negative response, is there any idea I can come up with that might turn it around? After hearing what respondents have to say unaided and asking for their suggestions, I believe a moderator should play an active role in the creative task of developing ideas, exploring new approaches. "What if it did . . .?" "What if they explained that . . .?"

If a group lacks animation, how can I get the members to loosen up and interact? Approaches: Have respondents stand up to look at materials on the table (gets the blood flowing). Break the group into smaller groups to discuss and take notes, either with people next to them or with people across the room, to change the dynamics. Take a five-minute break and have respondents stand up and stretch.

A touch of silliness can enliven the group

Have respondents change chairs, calling them by the old name cards in front of them, a touch of silliness that enlivens the group.

How do I make all the respondents feel free to express their ideas and reveal their personal behavior without fear of judgment from me or the rest of the group? Approaches: "We're interested in your feelings" (not "opinions," which are more intellectual). "People do things for all sorts of reasons." Reward revealing comments by saying, "I appreciate your honesty," letting other respondents know this is what you're looking for. Make comments like, "I see," "I understand," which provide support without suggesting agreement. When a respondent says, "I must be weird," be reassuring. You can say, "Other people have told me the same thing," or "There are many ways people feel about X."

When a respondent really irritates me or I disagree strongly with what's being said, am I keeping my feelings from showing and from affecting my learning? Keeping a poker face and an open mind is a challenge; so is not giggling at unintentionally funny remarks, such as a respondent's description of her kitchen's décor as "faux pas."

When real problems arise—a respondent is hostile, sick, drunk, or doesn't belong in the group (her cousin works for the competition)—how do I handle the problem quickly, nicely, and firmly without losing my relationship with the other participants? Approaches: Take a short break and check with your client. Sometimes I say directly, "I need to check on that." Ask the respondent to come outside the room with you or have the facility's host call them out. Say, "I'm sorry, a mistake was made in the recruiting—please come with me," and take the respondent out of the room. Explain to the remaining respondents that the person belonged in a different group, was misrecruited, or was clearly unhappy with the research. They'll probably be relieved. Ejecting a respondent is awkward, something I hate to do, but it can be necessary. If the respondent is drunk, be sure that the facility arranges some transportation.

Ejecting a respondent is awkward, something I hate to do, but it can be necessary

How do I stay fully tuned-in and open to new ideas when I have heard much of this before in previous groups or previous studies? Approaches: No matter how many groups you've done, there is always something new or something said in a new way. Confirmation of hypotheses is useful, too. If you've done a similar project a while ago, it's fascinating to see what has changed. For example, it used to be considered "weird" to eat cereal by hand out of the box for dinner; now, post-Seinfeld, it's a common meal.

How do I reach the level of unanalyzed impressions and emotions rather than intellectualized responses? Approaches: Ask questions that get to gut feelings, like, "What goes through your mind?" "What were you thinking at the time?" "What's the feeling?" "What's the mental picture you have?"

Talk, don't talk: managing the flow

Managing the flow of conversation entails two challenges: Getting people to speak up and getting them to shut up, so that everyone can have a turn.

Shut up!

I was brought up to be polite, so one of the most difficult aspects of moderating for me has been learning to cut off respondents. With the typical two-hour focus group and question-packed guide, time is tight. There isn't the luxury to allow long-winded respondents to go on and on.

Dominating respondents are a focus group bugaboo— and one of the main objections to using focus groups in the first place. These are the people who know it all (or think they do) who invariably answer every question first, who make others remain quiet and, worst, sometimes succeed in swaying other respondents. They distort the research process, becoming an obstacle to ascertaining individual opinions and creating a false impression of consensus. Troublesome respondents are not just annoying to the moderator and the back room clients, they also bother the rest of the group.

It's important to distinguish between a talkative respondent and a "dominant" one who influences others' opinions. Clients tend not to see the difference. Some respondents who have a lot to say are wonderful, expressing thoughts and feelings with vividness and clarity. They may stimulate more discussion. Other chatty respondents may be tiresome, but they don't hurt the group process. In fact, other respondents will sometimes purposely distance themselves from the loud mouth, making a point of disagreeing with that person. The chatterers, the bullies, the therapy patients telling of their woes, and the comedians making other respondents squirm do have to be managed. If the moderator doesn't take action, the group can be lost. So, early etiquette training aside, moderators must nicely, but firmly, get respondents to do what they have been instructed to do at the outset—to talk one at a time and to give everyone a chance to speak.

The nice-but-firm (NBF) approach is critical. Sometimes

Troublesome respondents are not just annoying to the moderator and the back room clients, they also bother the rest of the group there is pressure from clients to bring respondents in line right away. It's understandable that they want to get on with the group, but it can be a big mistake for the moderator to cut off respondents too soon or too harshly. As the session begins, the moderator is working to develop rapport with and among the respondents. They should be made to feel that what they say is interesting, that they are there for a purpose, and that they can enjoy themselves.

Being abrupt with a respondent during his or her first or second remark can send the wrong message to other group members: "You'd better be cautious or I'll do the same thing to you."

Most respondents do want the moderator's and group's approval. If they are pleasantly and subtly restrained, they tend to get the hint that their excessive talking is out of place. A man who eagerly jumped in first on every question until I held him back came over to me after the group and asked if he had been helpful; he hoped he hadn't talked too much.

The moderator's own feelings need to be dealt with, too. Let's face it, overly talkative or dominating respondents can be irritating. They get in the way of doing our job. They remind us of people we'd try to avoid at a cocktail party and here we are, shut in a room with this person for several hours. Plus, the client will become annoyed at us if we don't control them!

In some cases, an entire group can be rowdy and rambunctious with everyone talking at the same time. Or everyone wants to talk about his favorite subject. The topic is a magazine for adoptive parents and they want to tell in detail their stories about how they adopted their child. The topic is travel-related services for businesspeople, and they

Overly talkative or dominating respondents can be irritating— but they aren't necessarily "dominating"

focus on their feelings about airlines and airports, a subject of intense frustration for many, including me. Unless the moderator keeps the conversation on course, there will not be time to address the subjects the client needs covered.

Here are some of the NBF body language and verbal techniques I find useful for keeping individuals or whole groups in line.

For individual respondents:

Conductor or cop. One of the best pieces of advice I got on moderating was to use my hands as if I were conducting an orchestra (more subtly, of course). Respondents pick up on this non-verbal behavior. A hand up in a stop pose signals that they should wind up their comments.

No eye contact. Another non-verbal approach is to ignore the respondent. In the case of a talkative respondent to my immediate right, I literally turned my back on him, facing the other respondents instead of looking straight ahead. Since most people want to be recognized and realize they should be called on before speaking, this absence of contact bothers them. As they start to behave they are rewarded with recognition.

Certain respondents have a neurotic need to present their problems

Playback. One reason some respondents babble on is because they feel ignored in their personal lives. Certain respondents have a neurotic need to present their problems, or are undergoing a crisis and looking for moral support. Once, during the introductions of a group, a woman announced that her daughter recently had committed suicide. Letting these respondents know you've heard them and appreciate what they are feeling helps them stop. Sometimes a simple, "I understand what you're saying" is enough. Other times, it's helpful to demonstrate your comprehension through non-directive feedback: "So what you seem to be saying is. . . ."

A small pat. This works only with respondents seated close to the moderator. A light, reassuring pat on the arm is a warm way of saying, "I'm listening. I understand, it's okay for you to stop now," especially for respondents who are speaking of deep emotions. I don't recommend this for business sessions since a more professional tone is needed.

"Inadvertent" interruption. Breaking in after the participants have stated their main points—"Oh, I'm sorry"—usually works. The respondents sometimes even apologize. Such interruptions only can be used "innocently" once or twice in a session.

Yes, I remember it well. On occasion, one or even several respondents will start reiterating views they have already expressed. This repetition wastes time and bores other members of the session. A brief, seemingly offhand, "Yes, you mentioned that before," allows the conversation to move ahead.

Delayed response. To prevent the always-eager respondent from answering every question first, the moderator simply can say, "Let's have someone else go first," or "Let's start with the right side of the table." Another approach is to ask for a show of hands, "How many people have even visited that website?" then call on a respondent who hasn't said much yet. The eager talker will still have an opportunity to speak, but not to take over.

Flattery. A potentially serious problem in focus groups

occurs when levels of knowledge or experience vary sharply. Typically, the more informed respondents talk more because they have more to say or because they want to show off. The less informed feel stupid, embarrassed about revealing that they know little about the subject or, in some cases, they have never given it much thought. They have to be assured that it's important for us to know what people feel and what they know or don't know, that whatever impressions they have are helpful. One of the best ways of holding back the "experts," who may, in fact, be misinformed, is to recognize their greater familiarity with the subject. Ask them to wait until others have answered before responding to questions. They'll feel like they're on your side and cooperate.

Moving right along. Simple directness is needed sometimes with long-winded respondents. In these cases, simply say, "I need to cut in here," or "There's so much that we need to cover that we have to move on."

When everyone is talking, simply say, "Sorry, I can't hear you"

For the group as a whole:

Let's be brief. Prefacing a question by indicating time is short helps, especially with subjects we know people will want to describe at length. "Here's a topic that we could easily spend hours talking about, but we only have a few minutes. In a sentence, what would you say . . . ?"

Excuse me. When everyone is talking simply say, "Sorry, I can't hear you" or "I really want to hear what you're saying." The implied message is, "Help me out in doing my job, what you're saying is interesting" rather than "You're being a pain."

Not tonight. When respondents' eagerly discuss a tangential subject, the moderator can simply state: "We won't get to everything tonight." On services for business travelers, I once started out by saying, "We will be talking about many aspects of travel but not the actual flight. If you want to talk about that, you will have to come back and pay *me* to listen."

Help me. Chatty respondents who talk to their neighbors or entire rambunctious groups usually are sympathetic when you say, "I really need your help here. Let's slow down."

The tape. The focus group introduction includes informing participants that the session is being taped and that they should speak one at a time. They usually quickly forget, though, as they become involved in the discussion. It helps, at least for a while, to simply remind them that the tape is on and that it will be listened to later. With children, an incentive to speak one at a time is the promise that they can hear themselves on the tape when the session is over. With adults, humorous threats to make talkers "stay after school" and listen to the tape or threats of "no more cookies" are other ways to make the same point. These jokingly tell respondents they are acting like little kids without insulting them.

With adults, humorous threats to "stay after school" can bring back order

The gavel. When everyone is talking at once, I've sometimes joked about wishing I'd brought a gavel with me. When the hubbub reaches a point where such small jokes can't be heard, I've resorted to improvising a gavel and banging the table with a coffee mug, preferably empty.

Time out. Saying "time out" while positioning one hand horizontally across the other arm held up vertically (the football signal) helps in men's groups.

Yoo-hoo. Another simple hubbub-breaking technique is to wave and say loudly, "You remember me" or "Gentlemen/Ladies!" (said humorously). Usually this gets a laugh and brings respondents back to attention.

Total group involvement. Reminding dominant participants that "we want to give everyone a chance to talk" tells quieter members that their comments are welcomed—and expected. At the same time, the reminder does not have to be addressed to anyone in particular. This avoids embarrassing individuals and reinforces the need for the group to work together.

Changing their seats literally rearranges respondents' relationship in the group

Reseating. This is sometimes necessary with children's groups when two or more children chat together, or worse, argue and fight. If they don't respond to several warnings about being quiet, changing their seats literally rearranges the relationship in the group. Occasionally, adults repeatedly engage in side conversations. If necessary, the moderator can take a break and assign new seats to everyone. This avoids singling out the troublesome respondents.

Cooling off. Heated debates occasionally happen, sometimes over controversial political or social issues. A respondent also might see another's comment as an implied insult such as, "You can't be a good parent if you feed your children that product." Conflicts can erupt over even a seemingly innocuous subject, like the color of a package. Sometimes, for whatever reason, one respondent takes an immediate dislike to another, using him or her as a scapegoat, mocking or disagreeing with virtually any comment that person makes. There are moderators and clients who see such confrontations as useful in understanding both sides of an issue. My own feeling, however, is that the argument gets in the way of the group, preventing others from talking and making them uncomfortable.

You can talk about it later. On a number of topics, respondents want to talk about the subjects that interest them, not necessarily what you need to find out. For instance, on a project about information sources for automotive shopping, respondents were eager to discuss their shopping experiences and feelings about different makes. On a magazine about celebrities, we didn't have time to discuss the individual stars (not that I don't enjoy gossip). Ways of jumping out of these side excursions include, "Perhaps we digress," used for more upscale groups. "I know I'm going to frustrate you but in the interest of time, we need to move along; you can talk about it after the group."

Sometimes, for whatever reason, one respondent takes an immediate dislike to another

When all else fails

Most respondents and most groups can be dealt with through the NBF approaches. At times, though, more forceful techniques are needed.

Exasperation. This is a technique that's best reserved for repeatedly rambunctious groups. I was moderating a group of Detroit men talking about ceiling tiles — hardly a topic on which I expected much passion. They became exceedingly talkative, and wandered from the subject. I tried and failed to restrain the group several times. Finally, I was exhausted and in total frustration said, "Could we talk about the subject just for the hell of it?"

This directness seemed to shock respondents into remembering why they were there.

Confrontation. The moderator can be forced to deal very directly with a respondent's disruptions if the other approaches haven't worked. This is particularly true of the hostile respondents who hate the client's products or marketing in general. When a respondent stated, "I'm hostile to that bank," I responded, "Yes, I know and it's not helping the discussion."

Ejection. This most definitely is the technique of last resort, because it disrupts the session and can make other respondents worry about being kicked out. Some clients, however, are eager to use this approach if there is a respondent they dislike. On a number of occasions, I've heard clients relate stories of other moderators who threw a respondent out, clearly impressed by this show of authority. There are rare times when I agree that removal is needed—if a respondent reveals a close relationship with the client's competitor, is completely mis-recruited (a married man in a group of singles), or when a respondent has a highly negative effect on the discussion. There are subtle ways to handle this. Most often, the client or moderator on a break will ask the host or hostess to come in and ask the respondent to come out of the room. Telling the respondent she has a phone call still works nicely. Only if absolutely necessary should a moderator directly ask the respondent to leave. Depending on how obvious it is that the respondent has been asked to leave, I may explain to the group or simply move on.

The moderator can be forced to deal very directly with a respondent's disruptions if the other approaches haven't worked

Speak up!

So much for getting people to shut up. But what if you need to get them to start talking instead? Some focus groups — thank goodness not many — never come to life. Others may lose their energy toward the end. They're downright boring, and the moderator has to struggle to evoke any response. This can be because of the subject matter. Respondents find it uninteresting or they just aren't involved, especially if they're non-users, or the chemistry of those particular respondents may be less than ideal. In the case of 8:00 p.m. focus groups, clients will often attribute such blandness to the hour, but I don't find this to be true.

Some focus groups never come to life

Just as the need for "shut-up" techniques applies to individuals or entire focus groups, so do "speak-up" techniques.

Look interested. The moderator's body language has to tell respondents you really want to hear what they have to say, that they are interesting. I often sit on the edge of my chair and tend to scan the room to pick up on who wants to talk to me.

Mmm, mmm, good. One way to encourage respondents to keep talking is to make neutral non-verbal reassurances, like the sound, mmm. One client jokingly kept a record of the number of times I used this technique. I can't remember the number, but it was high.

Anyone else? After one or two respondents have expressed their views, if the room falls silent, a simple technique for getting more interaction is to ask if anyone else wants to comment. "Do other people agree or disagree?" invites more conversation and makes it clear that a diversity of viewpoints is welcome.

Shy respondents

need to be

invited in

Call on quiet ones. Sometimes shy respondents need to be invited in. They may, in fact, be waiting for the invitation. "Sam, tell me what you've been thinking?" Their body language may be a signal that they would like to talk. When an expression crosses the face, this can be used. "Alice, I see you nodding/shaking your head. What do you think?" A moderator I once observed addressed a respondent who had been silent for the first 15 or 20 minutes of the group, saying something like, "Bill, you've been shy." Labeling the respondent this way can be very embarrassing and have the counter-effect of making him withdraw further.

Circle the room. Going around the group to ask for respondents' comments is a way of calling on each participant without specifically pinpointing any individual. Similarly, respondents might be asked first to write down their reactions and then read them aloud.

Take notes. I try to either take no notes or a lot of notes, so people don't get worried about whether they're saying something "good" that I consider worth writing down. If I'm writing respondents' comments on the easel, I try to get down their thoughts fully.

Move around. While I don't jump on the table (don't know if I could), I do get up from the moderator chair and walk over to the easel to write down respondents' comments or walk to the other end of the table. Respondents have to look up. Even though they're still sitting, the energy of the room changes.

Stand up. Physical movement by the respondents can also be energizing. "This is the stand up and stretch portion of the evening" usually helps to get more reluctant respondents on their feet. "Come down to my end of the table" brings everyone closer together. Usually, this is done on the pretext of having respondents see some materials.

Physical movement by the respondents can also be energizing

Team time. Breaking respondents into subgroups to work on a question, such as brainstorming ideas for improving the product, alters the moderator-asks-the-question-respondents-answer dynamic. "Bring your chairs together so you can talk." This directive is another way of getting respondents to move around. Sometimes respondents who have been quiet up to now become lively.

Take a break. Most two-hour groups are run without intermission, but time out in a lifeless group gives the moderator a chance to think and consult with the client. A little caffeine for the respondents can be a good boost, too.

Ask provocative questions. In a group where respondents denied that television news anchors appearance mattered at all, I asked, "So, who's the sexiest one on TV?" "What's your biggest pet peeve about that store?" elicits an answer when a question about the store's negatives doesn't.

Try something—anything. Here's a great time to use some of these special techniques like sentence completion or role playing. "Pretend you need a computer and I'm the salesperson."

Help! Asking the group to help you out sometimes works. "I really want to understand why this product doesn't interest you."

Probe, probe, probe

Wouldn't it be wonderful if respondents answered questions fully, if they offered all the information needed for us to understand their motivations, perceptions, and beliefs? Even if they do respond in-depth, the answer may suggest more questions. Or you ask an open-ended question, and if it fails to spark a conversation or if you're not getting the deep, emotional responses that you want, you need to ask pointed follow-up probes.

Probes need to be:

Purposeful—always pursuing the study objectives

Personalized—picking up on respondents' comments

Punctual—keeping in mind how much time is left

Asking "why?" is

controversial

A probe can be as simple as the one-word question, "Why?" There's controversy over using "why" as a probe. Some people say that it's an aggressive or intimidating question. When your parents asked you, "Why did you do that?" they usually meant, "How could you have done such a stupid thing?" However, when a researcher asks gently, the question means, "Help me understand what motivated you to do that." I believe that a lot depends on the context and the moderator's tone of voice. Also, you can ask "why" in more words than one, which may soften the question. Alternatives include: "Tell me more about that;" "What do you mean by that?" "Can you explain what you meant?" "What was behind that?" or "What was your goal?"

Sometimes you will have to probe on subjects that are uncomfortable to discuss or those which respondents have never thought about and are at a loss to explain. In these cases, it's often helpful to switch from "you" questions to "it" questions. For example, rather than asking, "Why did you choose to wear purple today?" the question could be, "What do most people feel about purple?" or "What kind of message does wearing purple send?" or " If someone saw a person for the first time dressed in purple, what impression would he/she get?" This type of questioning takes the pressure off, and often draws out more information.

Examples of probes:

Tell me more: "What else did you . . . ?" "What did you mean by . . . .?" "So what you really wanted to do [voice drops off, respondent finishes the sentence]." "What were you thinking at the time?" "Can you give me an example of that?" "You said the [product] was 'nice' — what do you mean by that?" "How would you describe [the product] to someone who had never seen or heard of it?" "You said that expensive jewelry isn't 'me.' What's 'un-me' about it?"

Often, the first answers don't tell us very much

Tell me why: "Why do you feel that way? "What's behind that? "What was it that made you want to do that?" "Why do you think other people buy [the product]?"

Go beyond the obvious: Often, the first answers are the superficial conventional ones that don't tell us very much. For example, in one group respondents said that their choice of convenience store is based on location. It's a fair assumption that location is important and that drivers won't go out of their way, but with so many stores today, location is probably not the only deciding factor. These respondents might be asked, "What else makes you decide to go to one particular store?" "Is there a store you go to regularly?" "If two stores are both conveniently located, how do you decide which to go to?" "What brings you there?" "I've just come from Mars, so you have to explain what X means to people here." This approach asks respondents to explain what they consider the basics to a *real* outsider.

Emotions: "How does that feel to you?" "What's the worst thing . . . ?" "You seem to be annoyed — were you?" "What did [the product] do for you or mean to you?" "What thoughts and feelings come to mind?" "What do you associate with it?" "Think of a time when you felt that way and describe it to me." "Did it feel good or bad to you?"

Clarification: "Can you explain what you mean by that statement?" "I'm not sure I understand what you mean by that." "Meaning . . . ?"

"Give me some other words to describe that"

More "consumer language": "What's another way of saying that?" "Give me some other words to describe that." "'Convenience' can mean a lot of things; describe what this means to you."

I don't buy it: "Really?" "Earlier you told me you're retired now, but you just said you don't have time to read the newspaper anymore—what's the story?" "I've had other people tell me that they feel [the opposite way] —do you agree or disagree with that?" "Can you be more specific?" "Was there a time when you did that?" "How much time does flossing the teeth take? Are there other reasons why people don't do this besides lack of time?"

Checking hypotheses: "Several people said [X]. Do other people agree or disagree with that?" "What I seem to be hearing is [X]. Is that true or not?" "Is it possible that one reason for dropping the magazine was [x]?"

Check impressions: To keep people talking and to probe deeper, it's often important for them to know that you've heard them. With non-directive feedback, you play back what respondents are saying, using that as a springboard into a more detailed conversation or to move on. "What I seem to be hearing—correct me if I'm wrong—is that you're disappointed with the way the store has changed. Is that right?" Asked in a non-pushy way, respondents will freely say if they agree or not and explain why. Providing feedback is not the same as asking a "leading" question, which signals what answer the moderator wants (although some clients think so).

Devil's advocate: This enables me to push respondents to think and open up more, without pushing them to answer in a particular way. It's a non-leading, yet more active, form of questioning. "Playing devil's advocate here, why wouldn't people want this product, which saves them money?"

By giving respondents alternatives, they feel free to answer either way

Either/or: "Do you think X or Y?" "Is the experience pleasant or unpleasant?" By giving respondents alternatives, they feel free to answer either way. This is especially important if the group seems too eager to please, saying only nice things about the client.

Let's try again: If one question or probe isn't productive, the moderator needs to ask in a different way. The same issue may come up at several points in the group to get the "real" answer.

Make it better. Sometimes respondents are satisfied with a product or are hesitant to criticize. If questions about negatives and problems provide no information, ask how it might be improved or made even better.

A key aspect of the listening loop is thinking about what respondents are telling us verbally and non-verbally, asking myself if I understand its meaning. When I'm doing a group, I have an image in my mind of people walking toward or away from the product we're researching. Are they walking toward it quickly? Do they stop? Do they turn away, or do they stand still because they have no feelings about the product, or are they paralyzed by torn feelings? I listen for stories, for revealing comments that will help me "see" and "hear" this movie in my mind.

What respondents like about a product or service is its "convenience." What they like about a magazine is its "variety"— or they dislike the absence of these qualities.

Specifics make answers come to life

Vague answers really don't tell us anything. Worse, it is easy to make incorrect assumptions about the meaning of these common words. The client is left without an idea of what product changes are needed or of how to depict the benefits in advertising. Here are some examples of how probing for specifics can obtain vivid pictures that can be used by the client:

Moderator: What do you like about frozen entrees?

Respondent: They're very convenient.

Moderator: Convenience can mean a lot of different things. Spell out for me when and how they are convenient for you.

Respondent 1: I don't have to decide in advance what I want to buy for dinner. I can just open the freezer case ten minutes before we sit down and pick out tonight's supper.

Respondent 2: For me, the convenience is having everything in one container so I have fewer dishes and pots to wash. And I hate washing!

Respondent 3: Less time cooking means more time to spend talking with my family.

·   ·   ·

Moderator: What do you like about this magazine?

Respondent: It has a lot of variety.

Moderator: Maybe this sounds obvious, but why is that good?

Respondent: It has something for everyone.

Moderator: What do you personally get from the variety?

Respondent: I know that every week I'll find something new and exciting.

Moderator: Do you like all of the variety or some of it?

Respondent: Really just some of it. What I love is when they show all the awful outfits the big stars are wearing. They have so much money, but they can end up looking worse than I do. I skip over about half of the magazine.

When I hear something that makes that script fall into place, it's like hearing a "click." I love the movies and the theater, and at the point where we're getting to true emotional responses, it's a little like being in the audience. When you hear that something has clicked, you understand it—almost see it vividly. It's been brought to life.

I love the movies and the theater, and at the point where we're getting to true emotional responses, it's a little like being in the audience

The moderator's challenge

Perhaps the biggest challenge to moderators is the internal one. Listening while directing the flow of focus group traffic is one of the most important tasks of moderating. But you shouldn't just listen with your ears. The beauty of in-person research is you can learn not just from what respondents say, but also from their facial expressions and tone of voice. In the case of telephone depth interviews, listen for their tone, changes in rapidity of speech, and loudness.

The "listening loop" means that I'm listening to what I'm hearing, and thinking back to the hypotheses and objectives with which we've entered the project. I'm asking myself, "Are we hearing something that fits or doesn't fit?" That helps me to decide what question to ask next.

First, you start with listening with your ears. It's only through active listening that you'll be able to ask the most logical and meaningful questions and follow-up probes.

Listen for comments that are new. How do your respondents' ideas compare with what people were doing or saying even a few years ago? Try to pay attention to the individual remarks. In many cases, someone will make a "telling comment" that either encapsulates other research or suggests a new insight. For instance, one woman reacted to a commercial by saying, "I'm not a cute mommy. I'm a busy mommy." Her statement said a lot about the way many women see themselves. In a study of dishwashing, one woman said this was a romantic moment when she and her husband felt close, a disarmingly honest comment. This was certainly a different way of thinking about doing the dishes (not that it's inspired me to wash more).

In another focus group, a working mother observed that

there are "a lot of stressed-out kids today. We feel guilty and we spoil them with treats." Her comment suggested that there might be a good market for a variety of healthful snacks that little kids like and parents feel good about.

Look at which groups of people seem confident or defensive. These emotional responses can tell you a great deal about prevailing and shifting societal values. In 1970, working mothers were defensive because they were not home full-time. They often apologized for their need to make money. Then, as the number of working women rose, homemakers became defensive. It became common for a woman to introduce herself by saying, "I'm only a housewife," or more angrily, "I work, too." Homemakers felt criticized by society, other women, and even their husbands for not having an income or not being "interesting." Now, both working mothers and full-time homemakers can be defensive. This is a sure sign of divided values: many women can't make up their minds about where they belong.

The client's role

The client observers play an active role in the moderating process, too. Not only are they listening and watching, they can suggest new directions and add questions. During the session, I go back to the observer room at least once toward the end of the session to see if there's anything else the client wants to ask. Whenever respondents are writing or working together in subgroups, I also go back. Sometimes I set these situations up so I can disappear for a few minutes. In between sessions, it's important to get the client's feedback. What parts of the discussion are helpful, what should we spend more time on, what should we reduce or eliminate? It is not unusual for clients to give me more background at this time, filling me in on facts they hadn't thought to tell me about earlier.

The issue that arises is, how much control should a client have during the actual interview? Yes, they are paying for the research. Yes, it must serve their purposes. And yes, they almost always know more about the subject than the moderator does. However, clients who insist on intruding in the process can defeat the purpose of the research.

Clients who insist on intruding in the process can defeat the purpose of the research

Prior to the start of a new project, especially with a new client, I will tell observers that they will have an opportunity to ask questions and that I prefer that they do not send notes. Sending in constant notes is highly disruptive. Respondents know that someone is sitting behind the one-way mirror, but when a person enters the focus group room with a note, they often look surprised. They've forgotten that there is a third party involved beyond the group and the moderator. They may wonder, "Is the observer checking on the moderator?" Recently, after the third or fourth note brought in by the client herself, I turned to her and said, in what I hoped was a comic tone, "Go away!"

There are definitely legitimate times when a note should be sent. The client decides against revealing that they are the sponsor of the research or decides not to show certain materials—a switch in direction that the moderator cannot possibly anticipate. Or the moderator has given respondents incorrect information which needs to be changed immediately.

Notes are often unnecessary, however. They tell the moderator to move on just as she has done so, or they tell her to ask a question that is in the topic guide, before giving her a chance to do so, and so on. Worse, some of the notes are illegible or so long-winded that I have to stop in the middle of moderating and try to decipher what they are saying. By far the most maddening note I ever got was in a focus group where I was supposed to show respondents a series of products which might be put out under a major brand name, exploring whether or not each one fit. The note told me not to spend more than, I think it was, 4-½ minutes per product (I know the "half minute" part for sure). Was I supposed to use a stop watch?

Clients in the U.S. are, apparently, infamous in other countries for their desire to exert a strong hand in the focus groups. Just the fact that they usually attend all the groups is different. Whether this accusation is fair is difficult for me to judge, although the clients I have worked for from other countries have been less intrusive.

On the whole, having clients come to the focus groups is a good thing. They learn firsthand from what they see. I have their input on what they want to find out. I get more valuable information on what the project is about, and have someone to discuss the hypotheses with as the project progresses. Irritating and demanding as some clients may be, I prefer their involvement to conducting a study with no one present. The best clients are respectful of the process.

Moderating is a lot of hard work. It's also stimulating, exciting, fun, and it can provoke anxiety. At the end of a day of moderating, I feel wired and tired. The adrenaline is still pumping. I've usually learned a lot. I'm trying to figure out what it all means so I can talk with my client immediately after the group. I'm thinking about what I should do differently if there are additional groups. I'm thinking ahead to pulling themes together for my report. If only there were a way to turn that adrenaline off and get to sleep!

Irritating and demanding as some clients may be, I prefer their involvement to conducting a study with no one present

CHAPTER 7

Beyond the Basic Q&A: Special Techniques

A NUMBER OF SPECIAL research techniques can enhance the learning in focus groups, going beyond the usual "what are your feelings about" question-and-answer format. The popularity of some of these techniques stems in part from the search for more truth, the desire to "get beneath the surface" by liberating respondents to reveal more about what they really feel. During the course of a two-hour or longer group, special techniques provide a good way to vary the format and keep respondents interested.

Use what works,

not what is "in"

Another reason for the use of such techniques is the desire for novelty. Clients have asked me, "Do you have some fun questions to ask — new techniques — 'cutting edge' questions?" The veteran client observer may simply be bored hearing certain questions. For moderators, colorful techniques can be a good way to sell their services, showing they are creative and have "something new."

My own belief is that a moderator needs to know a wide variety of techniques, then use what works at the time, whether "new" or not. If respondents are giving rich answers, go with the conversational flow. Sometimes a question as deceptively simple as, "What is [the brand's] image?" can be very productive. Or perhaps a respondent offers an analogy to describe his mental picture of a product. In one recent group, a newspaper was spontaneously compared to a St. Bernard, signifying its strength and the loyal feeling the reader had toward it. A respondent may speak openly of his emotions, giving the moderator an opportunity to probe more, seizing a special moment in a natural way.

Several of the techniques described here can easily be used on the spot in a session without preparation. Sliding a question in may, in fact, be more effective than doing an elaborate set-up which can smack too much of, "Now children, we're going to play a game."

I have on occasion told a client I didn't want to employ a technique that I would resent if I were a respondent. One manufacturer wanted to start the group by my asking respondents to act out what it's like to be their dog when the food is put out for them. Possibly, this would have been okay later on, but I can't see beginning this way when respondents are still feeling awkward. At the same time, I realize that another moderator with a different personality might have pulled it off.

Several of the techniques described here can easily be used on the spot in a session without preparation

Advance assignments

Assignments done beforehand that respondents bring to the focus groups can serve as a springboard to the discussion. These give people a chance to reflect on their answers and to gather information. (We use the word "homework" among ourselves but, for obvious reasons, not in talking with respondents.) Once they begin writing down what they do, for instance, respondents become observers of themselves, more aware of their own behavior. It is not unusual for respondents to comment, "I never realized that I do X until I saw what I wrote." Doing certain exercises can save a good deal of time which can be used for discussion in the sessions. If a study involves new materials that require a half hour or more to go through, respondents can do this on their own, writing down their reactions individually. Written responses force them to think through their own feelings before hearing other respondents. The answers also have greater credibility to the client who can't dismiss criticisms as a result of group bias. Needless to say, the respondent incentive fee goes up for this preparation time. It's important to make sure in rescreening prior to the session that respondents really did complete the work before they are admitted to the session.

Some examples:

Product placement. After trying out the product, respondents are asked to fill out a brief open-ended questionnaire on overall reactions, likes, dislikes, and suggestions. For a new food magazine, respondents were asked to read the issue and to prepare one recipe.

Respondents are more specific when a real example is present

Disposable camera pictures. These can be of the respondents' lifestyles, for instance, what their living rooms look like, or photographs that depict how they feel about a product or idea. In an exercise for a footwear manufacturer, we asked clients to show in pictures what "comfort" means to them. Pictures are a form of observational research integrated into the focus groups.

Show–and–tell. Respondents can be asked to bring in objects to talk about — ones they like, dislike, bought recently, etc. Respondents are more specific in describing what they mean by vague terms like good or bad "quality" when a real example is present. It is also very helpful for the client to observe respondents seeing and touching the product. In a flannel sheet study, when one respondent complained about the "pilling," the client could feel how stiff the fabric was. We would not have guessed pilling meant scratchy or stiff. In a study to generate new ideas about loungewear, the client wisely decided to avoid using that term, which has narrow connotations. Instead, respondents were asked to bring in whatever garment they preferred for "relaxing in at home." It turned out that many items were far from the standard industry definition of loungewear.

Icebreakers. A technique some moderators use is to ask respondents to bring in a personal object, for instance, something from their home that has meaning to them. This may have nothing to do with the study's specific topic but serves as an introduction, revealing something about the respondent in an unintimidating way.

A time-use diary. These give us a better idea of respondents' everyday life. In a study of daytime soap operas, women filled in diaries of their activities over the past week (Monday to Friday during the day) both in and away from home. Were they not watching the "soaps" because they were busy outside the home? If they were home at a certain time, why did they choose to do something other than watch TV? If they watched a different program, why was that?

Product inventory. This is very helpful since it's so hard to

> **HOMEWORK EXAMPLES**
>
> ▶ *Read a magazine*
> ▶ *Prepare a recipe*
> ▶ *Take photos*
> ▶ *Keep a record of time uses*
> ▶ *List brands or companies*
> ▶ *List life changes*

remember what's in our closets or dresser drawers. For a bra study, respondents were given a form to fill in listing what they own, describing each garment and how often they wore it. Reasons why certain bras are no longer worn were also very helpful to the manufacturer.

Listing of brands/companies. For a study of brand loyalty, we asked respondents to list the brands that best "represent you" in over 20 categories (products, services and media); then to list brands that they "aspire to" in the same categories. The interviews probed what overall patterns respondents saw in their own feelings, and what these brand choices said about them. While, as expected, aspirational brands were usually more expensive than current brands, several people said the two columns were the same—they see themselves as "down-to-earth" people who reject luxury products.

"What's new" observations. For our special lifestyle studies, respondents are asked to make notes about changes they and other people they know firsthand are doing, thinking about and feeling. They are told to ignore what the media are saying. The questionnaire covers some specific categories, such as clothing, food/drink, media, and has room for any other observations. The focus groups probe what these changes have in common, what underlies them, and encourages speculation on where things are headed.

Projectives

Interest in projectives has grown dramatically in the last decade. While often called "new," this approach really is a return to earlier techniques. Projectives are indirect questions or exercises designed to elicit people's deeper feelings about a subject, the feelings they aren't aware of or deny. Some ask respondents to perform creative tasks, others to answer imaginative questions.

On the positive side, such questions and exercises can be very valuable. This is especially true when direct questioning does not seem to be getting at real feelings. For example, respondents may give highly "rational" opinions that appear to be masking emotions — the only reason they always buy a certain brand is its price; all women's magazines are alike; all deodorants the same, and so on. Projectives will almost always uncover new dimensions respondents overlooked or minimized. Used later in a session, when respondents are more comfortable with the process, these exercises can enliven a group.

Projectives should not replace direct questions, however. It's important to give respondents a chance to say what's on their minds on their own terms. We should not dismiss these top-of-mind or even rational responses as irrelevant. Early in one of the focus groups where I was a respondent, the moderator asked us to describe the research organization as a person. When another participant started saying what he thought of the association in a straightforward way, she cut him off and repeated her question. He backed off, unable to answer. It would have been better, I think, to let him express his thoughts, then afterwards ask the more imaginative question.

Projective exercises often require time and patience. They're not quickies. Initially, respondents sometimes feel awkward when asked what have been called "Barbara Walters questions" like "If the brand were a tree, what kind of tree would it be?" Sometimes initial topic guides have a projective exercise like collages, but clients become restless

Projectives are indirect questions or exercises designed to elicit people's deeper feelings about a subject, the feelings they aren't aware of or deny having

when it takes 20 minutes or more in the group. Having respondents do these as homework cuts down on the time, of course, but it may not be a good idea to tip them off to the topic. The question for moderators has to be, how much does the projective add to what respondents tell us? Are they open and revealing of emotions on their own, or is extra help needed?

Top- and middle-management types tend to resist exercises, which they see as treating them like children

Projectives — at least the more unusual ones — are used in consumer groups far more than in business groups. Top- and middle-management types tend to resist exercises, which they see as treating them like children. There are ways to ask some indirect questions here, too, however, by drawing (or appearing to draw) on respondents' professional expertise: If this product comes out, what kind of people do you think would buy it; why would they buy it; how popular would it be? If you had to write a history of the brand, what would you guess it to be? If you were the marketing director for the company trying to attract new users, what would you do or say?

Projective techniques:

Personification. A simple and popular question is to ask if the brand were a person, what kind of person would it be; this is repeated for several competitors. Would a Volkswagen be a man or a woman? What would its age, occupation, personality, hobbies and lifestyle be? What would it wear? Beyond this description, how would respondents feel about this person — what do they think it would be like to talk to a VW if they met it in real life, would they want to be friendly with it? Another personification question is, what member of the family or person you know would the brand be? There are obvious differences if respondents say a newspaper is their rich uncle, a kindly parent, or a best friend.

Two parties. Another simple question that often works: Imagine that there are two rooms outside; in one, brand X is having a party for people who are its fans and in the other is a party for brand Y's fans. How would you describe each party? What kinds of people are there? How are they dressed? What are the refreshments? What are people talking about? What is the atmosphere? What is the room like? Again, going to the next level of people's feelings, ask, "Which party would you rather go to?" In a study of soups where respondents played back the usual clichés about a major brand, they described it as having a polite, restrained party. The competitor's party was louder and more lively, lots more fun. One of the advantages of the party question is that respondents don't feel forced to come up with a single image of an individual user. However, if they answer that the party could have "every kind of person," that's too vague and broad. Ask, "What kind of people are most likely to be there?"

> **PROJECTIVE TECHNIQUES**
> ▶ *Personification*
> ▶ *Two parties*
> ▶ *Room imagery*
> ▶ *Guess who?*
> ▶ *Metaphors*
> ▶ *Fairy godmother*

Room imagery. Asking respondents to describe a brand as a room, complete with people, furnishings, atmosphere, and aromas, can also bring out deeper imagery. This is especially true of brands about which consumers have difficulty articulating their feelings, such as categories in which they consider all brands the same. Brands of rice and parenting magazines are examples. The second step, as with the exercises above, is to explore how respondents would feel in that room.

Guess who? If all you knew about someone you were about

to meet is that the person [gender not mentioned] uses brand Z, what else would you guess about that person? If you were standing behind someone on line in the supermarket and saw brand W in the shopping cart, what else would you guess?

Related questions are: If you could describe yourself only in terms of the brands you use or buy regularly, which brands would you mention? What do these say about you? What do they have in common? The answers can reveal a great deal about the respondents' personal values. Are they Levi's or Mercedes Benz guys?

If you were standing behind someone in line in the supermarket and saw brand W in the shopping cart, what else would you guess about that person?

Metaphors. These are the Barbara Walters questions that, jokes aside, can be very useful. Describing the brand as a car/vehicle and as an animal are two popular variations. Others include part of a meal, a movie, or a song. An article on the front page of *The New York Times* reported that focus group participants saw Presidential candidate George W. Bush as a Masarati.

Fairy godmother. What do people really wish for? For research on migraines, I asked the women what gift they would give a good friend who was suffering a bad headache right now. The gift could be a thing or something they do for their friend. An immediate answer in all the focus groups was, "I'd make dinner for her and take care of her kids so she'd have some peace and quiet." By talking about "someone else," the women felt free to express their frustrations and wishes.

Projective exercise examples:

User imagery photo sort. Respondents divide an array of

photographs into groups to portray how they see several brands. In a study of women's magazines, when respondents said that all the publications were alike, they chose very different types of women as the readers of the client's magazine and those of its major competitors. Photos that represent "your life now" and ones that show "hopes/wishes" for the future make it easy for respondents to reveal their lifestyles and aspirations.

User drawings. Respondents are asked to sketch a picture of the typical brand user, filling in the person's demographics (age, income, etc.), outfitting the person in detail, putting a meaningful object in the person's hand, giving the character a name, having the character make a significant statement, and so on. Since so many people are embarrassed about their inability to "draw a straight line" or even a crooked one, they need to be reassured that scribbling a stick figure is fine. (I usually demonstrate, putting them at ease immediately.)

Bubble drawings. Cartoons can be prepared in advance (or, if needed, sketched on the spot) depicting a situation. Respondents are asked to fill in the speech bubble of what each character is saying and a thought bubble of what the character really thinks. These two statements are often quite different.

Obituary/resumé. This exercise, also based on personification, asks respondents to fill in what the brand's obit or resumé would say (the second term is more comfortable for some people). An advantage of using this approach is that respondents will offer positives they might not have mentioned on their own, particularly of brands they criticize.

PROJECTIVE EXERCISES

▶ *Photo sort*
▶ *Drawings*
▶ *Obituary/Resumé*

OTHER EXERCISES

▶ *Free association*
▶ *Fantasy*
▶ *Sentence completion*
▶ *Mind-mapping*

Nightclub. A game board of a nightclub with different rooms —coat check, dance floor, balcony, mosh pit, etc.—is laid down on the table, and respondents are given cards with brand names. They have to work together to decide where each brand belongs.

Other written and verbal exercises:

Free association. This technique is so simple that we almost don't think of it as a technique anymore, but it remains an excellent way to elicit a wide variety of unedited perceptions and emotions: What comes to mind when you think of X, including thoughts, feelings, memories, images, people, etc? This can be done verbally so it goes more quickly. Used at the beginning of a session, it can be a good icebreaker. Another approach, typically coming later in the sessions, is to ask respondents to write down 6 to 10 words or phrases to describe one or several brands —how you would describe it and your feelings about it? Responses can be looked over by the back room observers during the session, highlighting some interesting answers for the moderator to probe further.

Fantasy. Finding out who people wish they could be is very helpful for advertising. The projective techniques outlined earlier provide some ways of getting at this. To probe women's feelings about sexiness, I asked respondents which well-known woman they would want to be for just a weekend. How would it feel to be this woman, where would you go, what would you do, what would you buy, what man or kind of man would you go out with? The short time period had a liberating effect. Respondents didn't worry about whether or not they would really want to be that woman forever.

Sentence completion. Respondents are given one or several sentences, which they are asked to finish verbally or in writing: The best thing about the product is. . . . The product makes my life better by. . . . Even after an extended discussion, this exercise often elicits new responses. Sometimes I'll simply ask a question trailing off at the end so respondents fill in the blank.

Decide/explain. A variety of exercises can be devised that ask respondents to write down what decisions they would make. The discussion then probes the feelings and reasoning behind the choices. Each respondent answers individually, before hearing what others have to say. Typically, they answer on a gut level, later reflecting on how and why they feel that way. A pretend shopping situation can be set up, for instance, with a mock retail display that respondents are asked to look at and write down their selection. To understand the "competitive frame" for diamond jewelry, for instance, we gave respondents a list of items and asked them to list their top three choices if they had $10,000 to spend. The list had practical items, like home repair, and other luxuries, including other fine jewelry. To understand newspaper subscribers' feelings about a particular section of the Sunday issue, we gave respondents a deck of cards with the names of the sections and asked them, on their own, to sort them into groups as they would read them. This instruction was purposely general, rather than establishing categories for respondents. The subscribers then told us where the section fit in their ritual and their feelings about it.

Mind-mapping. Respondents can do the map individually or as a team, passing the map around after each person has made some entries. This exercise takes more time since respondents have to be instructed on how to write a mind map, so I don't use it very often. (It is also a great way of making notes, because it allows the writer to spill out thoughts freely while organizing them at the same time.)

▼ *Mind map*

Subject: qualitative research

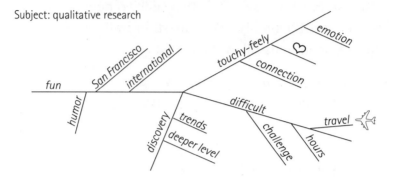

Sociogram. This is a technique I saw used in academic studies to understand relationships among people. I thought it could be applied to market research to explore people's feelings toward products or brands. Respondents put an X in the middle of a page of unlined paper to represent themselves. Then they are asked to draw a circle for each brand or magazine. The size of the circle indicates how important it is to them and the distance from the X indicates how close they feel to it. In the case of magazines, for instance, readers may feel that a publication is "important" to them (they need it for business or personal reasons) but that it is distant from them. Again, the ensuing discussion probes these feelings and relationships. This exercise does not force respondents to pick just one magazine as a "favorite."

Benefit chain or laddering. Another well-known technique, the benefit chain is designed to uncover what the true "end benefit" of a product attribute is to consumers. Starting with a product feature, such as "toothpaste has fluoride," respondents fill in two benefits of that to them, then two benefits of what they first wrote, and so on. The end benefit is typically tied to self-image—such as makes me feel attractive, because I don't have cavities. Rather than doing this formally, I often ask this question as a follow-up probe when respondents talk about a product attribute: What does it do for you? Or, the benefit to you is . . . ?

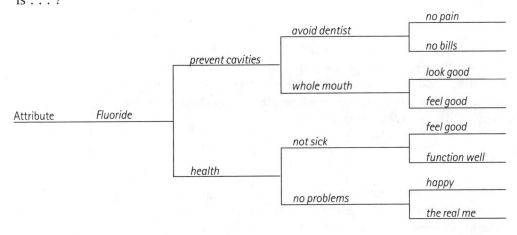

▲ *Benefit chain*

Role playing. Respondents are asked to act out a situation, playing themselves or someone else (another person or, as in the exercise I didn't use, a dog). The group can be divided into teams and given a scenario to work on. For example, "You're on a car trip with your family and you get a terrible headache." Alternatively, what I tend to do is ask a respondent a question like, "Pretend that I'm the furniture salesperson and you're the customer. What would you ask me? Now, what if you were the salesperson?"

By varying these techniques and choosing carefully among them, qualitative researchers can enliven sessions and probe more deeply.

CHAPTER 8

The Hardest Part: Analysis and Implications

I once got a report that had no structure, no purpose; it was just unreadable. This very skilled people person who did a good job in moderating could not communicate on paper. There was no analysis. Thank god I took notes. There was no way anyone not watching those groups could have reconstructed what we did.

—*Kathi Love,*
Mediamark Research, Inc.

It's amazing how **people who listen to the exact same thing interpret it differently.** What you think you've heard from a particular group may be something totally different from someone else.

—*Kathleen O'Shaughnessy,*
Unilever Home and Personal USA

INTERVIEWS ARE THE RAW MATERIAL of the research. Figuring out what the often chaotic information means can be the most difficult and challenging part of the process. It's simple enough for clients to observe the focus groups, even to get a transcript afterward, but they want and need more than this. How does the moderator, as an independent and objective observer, synthesize and interpret what has happened? Our role is to provide insights, then to suggest ideas and recommendations for next steps.

Analysis of qualitative research is far more demanding and frequently more confusing than quantitative research analysis. Many quantitative reports follow the question-naire, showing the table of results for a question without explanation. This doesn't work for qualitative research, since insights can come up at any point in the sessions. So many ideas surface in the course of just one group that moderators and clients feel their brains stimulated and, at times, overwhelmed by the bombardment. Sometimes a series of focus groups will be highly consistent—everyone hates the new concept—but they are rarely neat and tidy. Figuring out what we think the research means is often a complex task.

The word "moderator" ignores the analysis completely. Moderating is the public, visible side of our jobs. Report writing usually is the solitary side. Presenting—done for some projects—is again more public. Clients sometimes feel they have to trade off the analysis for the interviewing skills because it is so difficult to find qualitative researchers who do both well.

First impressions may be incomplete, but they are often both vivid and right

The debrief

The minute the moderator walks out of the conference room and into the back room, clients usually ask, "Well, what do you think?" which means, "How do you interpret what we just heard?" There are moderators who refuse to debrief immediately afterwards, declaring that first impressions can be misleading. While I agree that we may get additional insights and at times change our minds after more reflection, I think the immediate debrief is useful. First impressions may be incomplete, but they are often both vivid and right. If there are key ideas that are jumping out, I say so. If ideas are contradictory or blurry in my mind because I've shown oodles of materials to several groups in a row, I say that I have to sort things out.

The debrief should be an exchange of thoughts between the moderator—the person in the room with the respondents, the outsider who can be objective — and the observers, who are more personally involved, more knowledgeable and, most importantly, the people who have to make decisions.

An oral debrief immediately after the groups or within a few days is extremely useful. This can be done in person or by phone. In many cases clients are making quick decisions or moving into quantitative research. Now more clients are taking notes on their laptops during the sessions, issuing their own topline reports well before the moderator's. If the moderator is not involved at this point, clients may walk away with their own views, unbalanced by the impartial third-party perspective. A written report, issued weeks later, may be considered after the fact.

Research is more likely to be used when everyone discusses it

In the debrief sessions my role is both to present my top-of-mind impressions and to facilitate the discussion. This gives me a chance to compare my thoughts with observers' impressions. Their questions also help me know what issues to address in the report.

The research is more likely to be used when everyone discusses it, instead of just receiving a written report. Some qualitative researchers insist on a meeting both for this and marketing reasons. While I agree it is useful, I recognize the difficulties of getting the entire team together.

The multi-level analysis process

The complexity of qualitative research is what makes it fascinating, difficult and, ultimately, very useful. Just as the moderator's mind works on different levels during the focus group, we must look at different levels in understanding and reporting the research.

What happened: Reporting

The first level of analysis entails describing in some organized way what people said and did. This is essential but it's just the starting point. The simplest form of reporting is to play back what people said, using verbatim comments. Discovering "consumer language" is an important part of qualitative research. It was helpful for a web site to realize that most of their members, even sophisticated heavy users, did not know what an Internet "portal" is.

There may be an informal ranking here (very unofficial, without numbers), putting the most salient points first. These points can be the ones that provoked the strongest emotions and those mentioned most consistently. Things respondents said but didn't seem to care about would be given less weight.

Unfortunately, some researchers stop at this point. I've seen many qualitative reports that outline the major comments in a sentence or two of text with a few verbatims to demonstrate that someone did indeed make the point. In some cases, the verbatims can double the space of the text.

What it seems to mean: Analysis

Here there is more interpretation of body language and observation on areas of contradiction, and comments on deeper motivations. One of the most important tasks at this phase is to decide how to weigh what respondents have said. Were their feelings intense? Did they seem open to changing their minds given different information or are

Discovering "consumer language" is an important part of qualitative research. It was helpful for a web site to realize that most of their members, even sophisticated heavy users, did not know what an Internet "portal" is

they adamant on an emotional level? Sometimes there are reasons to suspect that respondents may not mean what they say. For example, they may have said they disliked a commercial, but they smiled while watching it. They may have said they disapproved of "sensationalism" in the media but could relate in detail all the latest scandals.

Differentiate between polite interest and real excitement: a lukewarm, "it's nice," vs. "I love it. Will you let me know when it comes out?"

Notice the way respondents present themselves. In a recent affluent market study, the upscale women in certain cities dressed in a sophisticated minimalist way, while those in another city wore clothing that was out of style and in poor condition. This isn't just interesting; it's useful for the client trying to understand who its target is.

Differentiate between polite interest and real excitement: a lukewarm, "it's nice," vs. "I love it. Will you let me know when it comes out?"

Be on guard against respondent clichés. They can be a trap in analysis. Veteran qualitative researchers often joke about their early days when they were misled by respondents praising a new product as good for camping out (not desirable in products other than camping gear); good for special occasions (to be used once or twice a year); good for someone else (women saying a product is for "bachelors," young people saying it is for "the elderly.") What this really means is, "It's not for me," which is anything but a compliment. Respondents' initial explanations of why they do or don't do any number of things often relate to "convenience," "money," and "time." These answers should not be taken at face value. What do these words really mean? Are there other factors that play a role?

Watch out for statements made for reasons of social acceptability. In general, people like to present themselves as honest, moral, rational. They tend to play down the role of greed, peer influence, sexual drives, and impulse. Certainly many people are motivated by the desire to do good and we should not cynically reject all comments along these lines, as some clients do. However, we need to look for patterns of consistency with a respondent's other answers and reported behavior.

The dynamics seen in the research can suggest where things may be headed in the future. Who's persuading whom? Are the Internet fans getting the non-users excited about the possibility of discovering more about the world? About saving money?

The researcher's comments and speculations that go beyond what was specifically said or done in the research can be very valuable — and should be clearly labeled. We can draw on our past experience in a particular city, for instance, or with a certain demographic group.

Qualitative research reveals how respondents subdivide into groups

How the market segments: Targeting

Here's where you look at who said what. The beauty part of qualitative research is that we can see how respondents subdivide into groups with particular attitudes or buying patterns. This helps the client craft ways to communicate with different segments and to design products for their needs. To use a fictitious example, you might be studying rice cakes and find that there are three segments of users. They are The Weight Concerned, who are eating rice cakes for weight control only; The Health Fans, who are eating them for good health, totally apart from calorie and fat concerns; and The Rice Cake Lovers, who eat them for their taste (yes, there are a few). Follow-up quantitative research is needed to find out the size of each segment.

Consumers can segment in various ways: along demographic lines like gender, age, occupation; and/or psychographically, based on their lifestyles or needs in a category. A store, for example, may appeal to both "trendsetters" and "lavish spenders" who may actually be behind in fashion. The difference between users and non-users of the product may not be income level but general shopping style. One affluent segment may love conspicuous consumption, buying the latest status car, while the other, believing in thrift and not showing off, chooses a value make.

What it means today: Trend context

The next level is to add the researcher's interpretation in the context of other research. Where do you think the market and trends are going in the future? Maybe the media (that is, broadcast and electronic media) are declaring magazines dead, but our research shows the very strong relationships people have with their publications. What is obvious to a moderator, because we've heard it repeatedly from respondents, may be new to the client. In the case of an office product that was positioned to make users' lives easier, high-level executives were concerned that it would add to their responsibilities. This suggested that there might be some underlying resistance. In the broader context of what we know about corporate life today, with streamlined offices and no assistants or secretaries, their concerns are very understandable. In one focus group, several homemakers declared that it is important to be "stay-at-home moms" through their children's high school years. Fitting in with our other research, these comments suggest that there may be growing support for mothers to take an extended

The difference between users and non-users of the product may not be income level but general shopping style

period at home beyond the pre-school years, unlike the prevailing view a few years ago.

How the client can use the research: Implications

This is the big "So what?" If I were the company president hearing these hypotheses, what would I do with them? As appropriate, discuss ideas for marketing, product development, advertising, promotions, pricing and so on. Do your homework so you're not naïve about your suggestions. A report I recently read discussed the possibility of the client advertising that its product is highly rated by *Consumer Reports*—but the magazine does not allow companies to use its ratings in their marketing efforts.

Thinking about the obstacles that either keep consumers away from a product or keep them from using it more often, what might overcome the problems? A good analysis not only lays out the obstacles, it looks for potential in a product or idea. Might the answer be as simple as providing new information? Changing the communication? Would a positioning change create more interest? What if rice cakes were presented as a filling breakfast for people on the run, for instance? Or is some deeper change in the product itself needed? By understanding the reasons for people's reactions and the bigger picture of trends and of consumer behavior, we can suggest ideas for the client to consider.

The report

In almost all cases, the moderator writes a report on a project. This may be the only document or it may be in addition to one or more reports from the client observers and

The report brings together in one cohesive document a record and interpretation of the study

possibly the ad agency as well. Frankly, reports are a lot of work, but I do believe they usually benefit the client. The report represents an independent perspective on the subject. It brings together in one cohesive document a record and interpretation of the study. Members of the research department, the marketing group, and the advertising agency who did not attend the focus groups can gain a picture of what was learned. People who join the company later on may also go back to the report for previous learning, and, as I mentioned, independent researchers working with the company later may use the report as a basis for exploration. If it is "just for the files" or just to make the client feel they got their money's worth, though, it's disheartening to write a report.

There are instances when the client does not want a report. They feel they can analyze the groups themselves. They may have a political point of view and don't want a moderator report that may present a conflicting opinion, or they want to save money.

Since actions are often taken quickly after the qualitative research, there is increasing pressure for qualitative reports to be delivered within days. This trend to greater speed makes our lives more difficult, needless to say, and many moderators I've spoken with are unhappy, believing that it hurts the analysis to rush.

Different types of reports are available for the client to choose from. These vary in length, amount of time needed and, of course, price. Longer reports simply take longer. (Names for report styles vary, but most moderators do offer options.)

■ **Topline report**—relatively short (usually 2 to 6 pages) and delivered 7 to 10 days after the last focus group. When there is a real rush, they may be done within 2 or 3 days. This may be sufficient to satisfy the client's needs, especially when the research issue is narrow. In other cases, clients want a more detailed report to follow.

■ **Summary report** — a somewhat longer discussion of the major hypotheses and implications in 10 to 20 pages, 2 to 3 weeks after the focus groups. While these reports give the flavor of consumer language, they do not have extensive verbatims (respondent quotations). In reality, there isn't always a clear demarcation between topline and summary reports in terms of length. In qualitative research, there can be a great deal to say about even narrow issues. (Toplines, however, are typically written in a shorter period of time.)

Clients can select the type of report they need

■ **Full report** — a more extensive analysis, with more individual examples, illustrative and interesting verbatims. Report length may range anywhere from 50 to 100 pages, sometimes longer. The quotes are often described as "bringing the research to life"—here is what people said in their own words, here are their stories. This type of report is especially useful in broad-ranging studies intended to give the client a basic understanding of a category or subject. Because it takes more time to transcribe comments from tapes, full reports often take 4 to 5 weeks and, needless to say, they are considerably more expensive.

■ **Presentation style report**—a bullet point report, usually in PowerPoint.™ Some clients find these easier to read and digest. This style also works well, of course, for in-person presentations. From the researcher's point of view, these reports are typically easier and quicker to write, but they may lack the flavor and vividness of a report in text. The time required for these reports depends on their thoroughness.

Reports have changed over the years. More clients are asking for shorter and/or bullet point reports. This fits the larger trend of time pressures. There is also more interest in graphics and charts to summarize qualitative hypotheses. Photographs showing the respondents and materials presented also literally give readers a vivid picture of the research.

Report writing: A to Z or patchwork quilt?

It sounds logical to write a report from the beginning to the end, with these sections:

- Background and Purpose
- Method
- Summary and Implications
- Discussion
  - First chapter (e.g., general overview)
  - Second chapter (e.g., the product category)
  - Third chapter (e.g., the client's brand vs. competition)
  - Fourth chapter (e.g., new concepts)

And it seems logical to write each section from beginning to end.

I don't think I've ever done a report that way. Some other qualitative researchers tell me they do; others say they don't. It used to bother me that I couldn't write in a straightforward way from A to Z. Now I accept that my mind doesn't work that way. Writing the introductory sections outlining the research's background and purpose and the methodology is usually easy enough. Sometimes I write them first, sometimes later.

Every researcher has her own way of writing. I'm not recommending my approach. Do what works for you; if your way seems "weird," that's okay. In case it's helpful, here's a picture of my patchwork quilt method.

STEP 1: *Write about the themes that stand out.*

For the discussion section, I usually work on each "patch" as inspiration strikes, that is, as a theme comes to mind. I do whatever is most salient first, eventually getting around to the more difficult pieces. When I write a new piece, I may modify a previous one. I make notes to myself in my draft as a reminder: [MOVE?], [CHECK], [FILL IN], [FIX], and so on. It's better, I've found, to get an idea down and work on the wording later rather than to fuss over the crafting as I go.

A simple way of organizing is to write a brief overview on a topic (a store's image was very strong), discuss positives, then discuss negatives. This gives the client an overall sense of what emerged, followed by specific points that can be enhanced or communicated in the future, and weaknesses that need to be addressed.

STEP 2: *Check notes and transcripts.*

After I've finished the preliminary first draft, I check my notes or transcripts to see what I have left out or gotten wrong. It sounds more logical to review notes first, but I found I became overwhelmed by small details; the reports took far longer and weren't any better. The more I've done qualitative interviews, the more I have come to trust that the points most prominent to me are the ones that are important. These provide the base for the report

Step-by-Step Report Creation

STEP 1:
Write about the themes that stand out

STEP 2:
Check notes and transcripts

STEP 3:
Sew the pieces together

STEP 4:
Write the Summary and Implications

STEP 5:
Careful proofing and reading

(the backing the patches will be attached to, to continue the quilt analogy), with refinements coming later.

STEP 3: *Sew the pieces together.*

This is the editing process—shuffling the order, revising to make points clearer, smoothing out the writing style.

STEP 4: *Write the Summary and Implications.*

I almost always save this section for last, after I've pulled all my thinking together. And I write the type of summary that seems appropriate for that report, a condensation of the discussion section with the ideas and recommendations at the end, or summary with the implications after each point.

STEP 5: *Careful proofing and reading.*

It's impossible to do a good job proofing your own report

Always get someone else to read the report. It's impossible to do a good job proofing your own report. Spell check is absolutely essential (amazing how many people don't take this step) — but it's not enough. Too many grammatical and spelling errors slip through that good human eyes will catch — including spelling the client's name and products correctly! If the reader doesn't understand what you're trying to say or had to read it three times, you probably need to rewrite.

Report dos and don'ts

Make reports readable. A good qualitative report should be journalistic in style, understandable and interesting to non-researchers. Clients shouldn't have to work hard to understand what you mean or find the report boring. (At the same time, our writing doesn't have to be at the level of *The New York Times* or have to "hook" a reader from the first paragraph.) The subject may sound mundane, but the report can still be interesting because it provides insights and tells a story. The final test of a good report is simple: would you want to read it?

The final test of a good report is simple: would you want to read it?

Remember writing basics. Vary sentence beginnings — "respondents said" (including "most respondents," "some respondents," "a few respondents") at the start of a sentence or paragraph quickly becomes boring. Keep in mind good grammar (verbs agreeing with subjects), proper spelling (it's and its, their and there are constantly misspelled these days), and correct punctuation (in the U.S., periods are inside quotation marks). Make your writing concise and crisp. Don't try to be cute. (I especially dislike "folks," "gals," "moms"—words I've seen in a number of qualitative reports.) Don't try to sound pseudo-scientific, treating respondents like guinea pigs (instead of "males said," write "the men said"). Don't try to impress the marketing managers by sounding like an MBA (even if you are one). Don't try to impress the academics.

Recreate the experience. A key purpose of a report is to bring the research to life, especially for those who didn't attend the focus groups, giving them a picture of the human experience. The goal is for readers to gain an intuitive feel for their customers and prospects — what they are about, how they think and feel.

Do more than just report back. Explain and analyze what

respondents said; don't present it undigested. Findings and verbatims are the foundation for implications and next steps, not a substitute for them.

Place what you've learned in context. Only one respondent made the comment in this study, but you have heard it repeatedly elsewhere; it fits a pattern. Without revealing proprietary information from other studies, it's important to show the client that this is not an isolated instance.

It's surprising how often researchers leave out an issue the client wanted explored or ignore some materials presented

Address all the client's objectives. If it's in the objectives, it had better be in the report and implications. It's surprising how often researchers leave out an issue the client wanted explored or ignore some materials presented. That introductory section isn't just for the files — it's a checklist for us to cover.

Organize the report by themes. Don't follow the topic guide sequence. Rather than first discussing attitudes, then behavior, for instance, talk about the role of price shopping, which combines attitudes and behavior.

Don't write the report focus group by focus group. Again, it's our job to put things together. Discuss the overarching themes, pointing out differences that came up among segments (users vs. non-users), by demographic group (men and women), or by geography. If the segments are very different, it may be useful to have an overview section at the start that makes the point, then go into a general discussion.

Don't report back on the answer to each individual question. If you ask a series of projective questions (what animal would the brand be, what part of the house, what celebrity, etc.), don't do a blow-by-blow. What did you learn from the answers—that the client's brand is seen as trustworthy, as wimpy, aggressive and nasty, or what?

Do talk more about what's new — surprises, what the client didn't expect. Spend more time discussing and explaining hypotheses that go against the client's thinking and current marketing approach. These are points that clients may resist; you have to try to communicate them more persuasively. A report is a conversation with the client: here's what I learned and want to tell you.

A report is a conversation with the client: here's what I learned and want to tell you

Don't belabor the obvious. What the research confirmed can be said briefly. Mothers care about their children's nutrition. Convenience stores are convenient. Pet owners care about their pets, and so on. These points may need to be made, but they can be made quickly so readers don't feel they've wasted their money on the research.

Don't just state the overall "finding." What we hear in the qualitative research may or may not be borne out in a statistical survey. The purpose of the focus groups is not (only) to find out whether consumers love or hate a new product concept, for instance. It is to understand the dynamics and the diagnostics: Why do they love it or hate it? What are its strengths and selling points? What are the issues that need to be dealt with in terms of the product and/or its communication?

Go beyond the words. What people said is just the starting point, as I've said repeatedly. Unconscious motivations below the surface may come out which we should comment on. Americans often deny they care about status, for instance. It is not unusual, however, to see a respondent literally posturing with his or her nose in the air talking about a possession and showing off pride in ownership.

Don't show actual numbers. Ten people said this, four people said that, or half the group said this. This is not what qualitative research is about. As the report caveat says, the sample is small and may not be projectable, the questions are purposely semi-structured. Focus groups, no matter how many were conducted, do not constitute a "survey." Including numbers implies the research is larger and more cut-and-dried than it really is. The danger is that some clients take these numbers literally. While it may seem like a small matter, I never say "many" respondents because even that can be misinterpreted as a large number in general. However, "many" moderators do seem to do that. Instead, use words like most, several, some, a few, only one. For the same reason, don't imply that what was seen in this study applies to a broader market. "Women said that they loved rice cakes" implies all women feel that way. Better is "The women interviewed [or "the respondents"] said they like rice cakes."

Pay attention to individual comments. It's easy to look mainly at the overall direction of the research and to overlook the remarks of just one or two respondents. Not only to these comments add "color" to the report, they can be invaluable in stimulating insight and sparking new ideas. In a jewelry study, respondents often said a reason they are reluctant to buy is that they worry about losing expensive pieces. One woman said she had solved this problem by buying earrings with screwbacks that stay on — a nice, simple solution that is worth studying further. In an employee study, the client was considering a new internal slogan after a period of downsizing: "All Together Better." One respondent sarcastically paraphrased the line as "all together bitter," a "red flag" that the slogan could backfire.

Go beyond the issues. If you learned something useful in other areas, say so. "Bonus insights" are an extra value.

Learning from bad examples

Here are examples from real reports (with details disguised), why they don't work, and ideas on how you can make them better.

Example 1:

> **The main factor in respondents' choice of a bank is convenient location. They also want a bank that is accurate in its customer statements and that provides good customer service.**

Yawn. Does this paragraph tell you anything you would not have known without having done the research? On the one side, it seems obvious that people want a convenient location. However, today many large banks have branches almost everywhere. How do customers choose among banks that are equally or almost equally convenient in location? With the rise of ATM machines and now online banking, is convenient location as important as it once was? Accurate bank statements are desired in a bank, but are they the deciding factor in choosing a bank (customers don't know in advance who's accurate) or in staying with a bank? "Good customer service" is vague. What specifically does it mean? The client needs specifics that are operational, that can be turned into practical actions, not generalities.

Better would be:

Convenient location remains extremely important to customers, as would be expected. In particular, they want a bank with branches close to both work and home. This has implications for the location of new branches near office and residential neighborhoods.

Certain attributes are considered the basics of a good bank, such as accurate customer statements that are easy to read. According to respondents, many banks do not provide such statements. In fact, errors are sometimes a reason for switching banks; the problem is not just the inaccuracies but a bank's slow action to remedy the statement. On the positive side, customer service that is seen as superior can lead to strong loyalty. This includes both personal service (a warm hello when the customer speaks to a teller, apologizing for mistakes) and electronic services (such as online transfers). A segment of customers places a high priority on personal service, while others are happy to have as little interaction with people as possible.

The second version is better because:

- It's more interesting
- It gives some new insights
- It gives some flavor of different types of people and segments
- The client gets a more specific idea of what customers are looking for

Example 2:

A chart about a facial product that appeared in a report:

LIKES	**DISLIKES**
Convenience	Dries out your face
Ease of use	Too rough
Works fast	
The medication	

That was it—no further explanation. Huh? This would be okay as a summary chart, but without any interpretation by the researcher, it's hard to know what to make of this. Does the product have an unpleasant feel for users, or does it arouse a fear that it's ripping the skin, that it's bad for them? Is convenience different from ease of use? Does it mean saving time, saving effort, or that the product is uncomplicated? Give me some meat, something that's specific.

Better would be:

Strengths of the product included:

The medication — the fact that it contains XYZ, which promises to treat the actual cause of acne so it doesn't come back, was very important to the teenagers. This gives them hope that they won't have a "face full of zits" just days after a pimple has cleared up.

Convenience — the pads are quick and easy to use, then can be thrown out. This is considered much more pleasant, cleaner, and more effective than the old-fashioned washcloth method.

Quick results — while teenagers would love to have a product that "zaps" their pimples "instantly," they are happy that the product helps them within days. Their complexions look better the next day and the pimples are gone two days later.

Example 3:

The girls prefer McDonald's, Red Lobster and Olive Garden. The boys' devotion is split among three brands. McDonald's (received three votes) Olive Garden (received two votes). The boys' average score on the ad for McDonald's was 7.4.

"Devotion"?? Are teenage boys *devoted* to their fast-food restaurant, or was the writer just trying to be colorful? Why give out specific counts in qualitative research, especially just one focus group? No one brand was preferred among the boys; the three were about equal. Give analysis, not numbers.

A big part of analysis is looking for patterns, themes, and areas of agreement, but it's about insight, not about consensus or numbers. One brilliant comment can illustrate, illuminate, warn, or spark ideas.

Part 2
Learning from Experience

CHAPTER 9

Mantrack: A Case Study in Qualitative Trend Detection

Adapted from a paper written by Judith Langer and Terri Bunofsky,
Playboy Enterprises, 1998

THE USE OF QUALITATIVE RESEARCH as a trend detection tool has become a trend in itself over the last few years. While qualitative research was once used mainly to answer specific questions about a particular category, it is now being recognized as a valuable tool for seeing the big picture of consumers' lifestyles and values. *Playboy*, as a leading men's magazine, has monitored men's attitudes and behavior across the decades, using quantitative research. In 1998, *Playboy* decided to use qualitative research for its study of key areas of men's lives: career, family, self-image, relationships with women, and leisure. They were also going to study some "hot" areas: privacy and technology.

Why did *Playboy* go with qualitative research? Like many other clients, they were interested in using the results as a preliminary step to conducting a quantitative study. Qualitative research allows for hypothesis development and provides questioning language for the quantitative survey. They were also interested in using "sound bites" from the groups and visuals to enliven their presentations to advertisers. After all, when people are entertained, they pay attention a little more closely to what you're saying. And because they were interested in creating "buzz" in the media and in the advertising community with the results from their research, they knew that they needed to get men to "open up" in a way that a straight-forward survey alone would not have accomplished.

Once they decided on qualitative research, focus groups were chosen over one-on-ones because of their dynamics. We risked "group think," but thought the interaction and honesty would outweigh this possible problem.

Why did *Playboy* choose me, a female, for a moderator? Some might think choosing a female moderator to speak with men about relatively personal matters a bit risky. But there were several potential advantages to using a female moderator older than the respondents:

Men are not going to compete with a woman while they sometimes do with another man.

Men feel a greater need to explain their feelings and actions to an "outsider," not assuming that the moderator already knows firsthand.

Men are more likely to view a female moderator as "motherly," accepting, and non-judgmental. The moderator's age also removed the sexual tension that might have been present with a young female moderator.

Indeed, the men in the groups felt free to speak their minds, to the point of voicing sexist views without inhibition.

The guys

There were several different ways we could have split the groups: by age, marital or relationship status, presence of children — all very important to men's lifestyles and outlooks. The ultimate decision was to split the groups on the basis of age. This would give us a clearer picture of generational differences and increase the comfort level the men would have in the discussions. Seven sessions were held, divided among men in these age groups:

18–24, *young adulthood*

25–34, *settling down*

35–49, *settled down*

These groups included singles and married men, men with and without children, and men in different occupations. The groups were held in St. Louis, Dallas, New York, and Los Angeles.

One additional group was held in Manhattan, with so-called "trendsetters" — men aged 18 to 29. A good deal of trend research today involves studying people who are ahead of mainstream consumers in creating and "adopting" new ideas, behaviors, and products. To find trendsetters, respondents were screened as "trying new things early on" in several different areas, going out frequently and seeing themselves as being "ahead on trends" generally.

While the other sessions went well, the trendsetter group bombed. The men never connected with one another and shared relatively little information. What went wrong? Several guesses: The 18-to-29 age group ranges from students to men married for several years and already fairly advanced in their careers.

"Trendsetters" turned out to include men who were "trendy" in very different ways — from being into the downtown club scene, on one side (quite literally), to working on Wall Street and smoking cigars in the uptown restaurant scene, on the other. Worse than having nothing in common, the two segments disliked each other.

The questions

We started off with a six-page topic guide that began with some general questions, then moved to a number of specific probes about the areas of interest for the study. We knew it was too long, but it was intended to be just what the term "topic guide" says, a guide on topics to cover in a free-form way. We also went in armed with several projective techniques—a photo sort on role models, a "self-pie" in which respondents drew a pie chart assigning percentages to the satisfaction they get from the various aspects of their lives, and materials for a collage on men's lives in the 1990s. Use of these techniques was based on the theory that they might help respondents reach a deeper level, bringing out ideas the men would otherwise feel hesitant to talk about.

After the first two focus groups (unfortunately, one of them with the uptight trendsetters), we pretty much scrapped the topic guide. The projectives were not needed. In the focus group where the men were willing to talk, they spoke vividly about their feelings and observations. In the focus group where they weren't, the projectives didn't really help. For instance, the role model question, asked directly, was more productive. In answer to the question, "Who do you admire or respect and why?" the men gave diverse and sometimes surprising answers, including Michael Jordan, Tiger Woods, my father, even my mother, and God. (We did not use the term "role models" since respondents often deny that they have any.)

Our new approach was, on paper at least, far simpler. [See Figure 5-2, p. 101]

Trend teams

After the men's introductions, the respondents were divided into three subgroups, working together to come up with a list of "what's new and different among men in your age group" that they see (not just hear about through the media). This approach asks respondents to draw on their own personal experience and to be a "social reporter" observing their peer group. They were told there didn't have to be consensus, to put down everything that was said. The teams helped respondents break the ice and get comfortable with one another. Each team reported on its ideas, which were listed on an easel.

In some groups, the discussion began with whatever trend respondents wanted to talk about. In others, a starting point was chosen from the respondents' initial list.

Probes included:

What is the trend?
Why is it happening?
What does it say about where men are today?
What ties the different trends together?

Themes brought up in previous groups were explored further. This is the part of the trend-detection technique that looks the easiest, yet in some ways is the hardest, requiring quick judgments on what will be productive and interesting for the study.

A conversation, not an interrogation

The moderating approach was highly conversational, picking up on respondents' leads, asking them for their thoughts, and for specific examples. In a sense, it was more like group therapy than a structured interview that respondents would feel was following a written outline.

Kindness to dead horses

After tries in a few groups, we decided to drop the subject of privacy. No one seemed to care, even when hypothetical problems were described. For example, a list of all the videos you ever rented is given out. Respondents were clearly bored. The horse was truly dead; no point in flogging it further. (Despite this, we cautioned in our report that privacy could well become an issue in the future if events made people more aware of the dangers to them personally.)

Opening up and closing up

Toward the end of the groups, when the men already knew one another well, they were asked to write down answers to a three-part aspiration question, "what I aspire to be, to do, to have." Then they were asked to discuss what they wrote. The men gave open, rich, detailed, thoughtful, and sometimes surprising replies.

The answers

Here are a few highlights of what we learned:

Role turmoil

Relationships with women seemed to be treacherous territory today for all three age groups. While the media talk about role confusion, what we found was not uncertainty but resentment that women are in control of many areas of men's lives. Women call the shots in the workplace—men have to watch everything they do and say to avoid claims of harassment, but women can do whatever they want. Women employees have their travel schedule reduced because of family responsibilities, but men can't. Women are the style-setters in clothing, even responsible for reviving the chicness of cigars.

Women's sexual aggressiveness is seen as a mixed blessing. It's great that women admit they're "horny" too, some men said. Others, though, were downright uncomfortable.

The men split, too, on the role of working mothers. The traditionalists complained that many mothers today work only so the couple can pursue selfish and petty materialistic goals. Modernists, though, said that they don't want a wife who just stays home taking care of the family with no other interests—"that's a mother, not a wife," not someone they can talk to.

The discontent of the men in the Mantrack study stood out in part because of the contrast with a study that we conducted around the same time for *Redbook* among married women aged 25 to 42. Certainly, the women also talked about modern pressures. But the overall tone was far more upbeat, even exhilarated at times. While a number of men (married and single) think their relationships with women have gotten worse, the women in this and other qualitative studies see improvements. Both sexes, interestingly, attribute the changes to role expansion by women. Couples today were described by the women as having relationships of loving independence. There is partnership power, with both members playing major roles in decision-making for the family, in contrast with the past when the man was the sole ruler.

Rush-seeking

Many of the activities the men described fit into a pattern —the search for excitement and, for some, the desire to take risks with the ultimate goal of feeling a "rush." The trend cuts across age groups, though it takes different forms:

18-to-24-year-olds: more involved in heavy drinking, drug use (including heroin, which they defend as "cleaner" now), unprotected sex, extreme sports with its "danger element" (bungee jumping, drag-car racing, snowboarding, etc.). Significantly, the men themselves sometimes disapprove of their own behavior, especially drugs.

25-to-34-year-olds: some look for the rush in sports, including competitive, aggressive ones, like target shooting and paint ball. Both under-35 age groups love the vicarious thrills of computer games.

35-to-49-year-olds: less physical, turning to excitement in activities like gambling.

Golf, trendy all over again in all the age groups, is another safe, socially acceptable outlet for aggression which produces a thrill.

Underlying this trend is men's eagerness to get high, to feel the adrenaline rush of the risk, to experience something new and exciting, to party, to relieve stress, to break out of boredom, perhaps to forget what's bothering them. Rush-seeking seems to be a combination of old and new— the usual male competitiveness along with response to today's pressured environment. Because of the intensity of needs wrapped up in this trend and the many forms it takes, we believe that it will be around for a while, expressing itself in a variety of novel ways.

My father, myself

Despite the anger about role reversals, despite the fairly wild acting-out behavior of several men, most of the men expressed the dream of having a happy home life. They want marriage and commitment, and they want to be a good husband and father. They spoke of these goals with strong feelings, often quite touchingly. Importantly, too, some who are already fathers have taken steps to be more focused on the family—their wives were staying home or the men who were fathers had taken less demanding jobs.

The transcript

What follows is an annotated excerpt from the actual transcript of the Mantrack focus group with Dallas men aged 18 to 24. The purpose of including this excerpt is show an example of conversational probing and to illustrate the honesty and great quotes that often come from focus groups.

"R" indicates a Respondent. Bolded comments were made by the moderator. Comments in brackets are intended to help the reader understand the purpose of a particular probe or to give insight into a particular answer.

[After respondents work in separate groups on what "new things" they see happening in their age group]

We are going to go back and forth. Why are these things going on, what's different? Kyle, you're the notetaker; you want to give me one?

R: Well, the first thing we had on our list here is something I'm not proud of, but a lot of men our age now are doing drugs. I don't know if it's just to get that quick fix, what it is, just to hang out.

R: A lot of them are doing it just for fun; they just think it's fun.

R: Or just to be noticed.

R: A lot of my friends smoke dope, and the reason they say is it's a quicker high than drinking.

R: I got a 14 or 23 on the SATs, I smoked the whole time in high school, and whenever I didn't have anything new to smoke, I couldn't function. I'm an ADD, so it's just like I need it to stay focused and chill in class, I had to smoke. I just kept that between me and my family, but it actually helped, yes.

R: It's more social than it is, just a couple of friends just smoking a joint.

R: Harsh drugs—heroin and LSD.

R: Not everybody, but there is a group.

R: It's everywhere.

R: It's not just Plano, it's not just Dallas—it's all over.

R: It's rich people, if you're yuppies up here.

R: It's cheap.

Richer people?

R: It's rich people, it's your yuppies.

R: I wouldn't generalize it like that because I'm 21 years old and me and two of my friends have a house in West Plano. And I throw keg parties every two or three weeks. I have parties and it shows up. And I kick people out of my house and I have no problem calling the cops. I have no problem with marijuana being smoked in my back yard or my garage because that's just—you can't keep that away. But when somebody comes over with cocaine or heroin — and it shows up — and you'd be amazed at the people that it shows up with.

R: You could have a multi-millionaire family and their youngest child's doing heroin.

R: It's a very inexpensive drug and it's a quick high.

R: It's different than it used to be. Heroin used to be — it was dirty, you shot it up — and now it's a totally different drug.

How is it different?

R: It's cleaner. You snort it.

R: You can get it in powder form or you can shoot it up.

Not shooting it up with a needle?

R: Most of these kids that have been dying — and most of the people that I know or heard of who are doing it or trying it, they don't want to get into shooting up. Not at first. They snort it now.

R: And then after that rush when you get used to that then they shoot it up.

R: Then they shoot it up. The rush is gone.

R: The way people are dying in Plano — the last girl that died, she was a close friend of mine. Some guy stuck her in the leg with a needle. And she was previously during the day snorting cocaine and smoking weed. And when you mix the two of them together — heroin's a depressant, coke's sort of like an up step.

R: Speed.

R: It's got a little bit faster beat. It confused her brain and her brain just slipped.

R: Like he was saying, he didn't mind if people smoked

marijuana in his yard or garage—I don't really catego-
rize marijuana as a drug. Because everybody I know—I
can't say everybody—95% of the people I know my age
smoke marijuana.

R: It's been used for like 10,000 years. It's been used for
health —

R: Used in medicine—

But heroin is different?

R: Yes. Because the worst thing . . .

R: You can't get addicted to marijuana.

R: Not physically.

R: Heroin's real different.

R: Marijuana's never killed anybody.

R: If a husband goes home and smokes a joint, the worst
thing that's going to happen—he's not going to beat his
wife—worst thing that's going to happen he's going to
eat her dinner. It's just to relax, I believe.

R: I went to rehab for heroin. And it really sucks. I've been
—just drinking a little bit of beer here and there, taking
like random drug tests that my parents give me. And
you get into that kind of trap then it ruins your life.
Luckily I had the chance to get it all back and I got my
shit together.

R: Good for you.

*[Use the "outsider" role to probe—older generation yet not judg-
mental]*

**When I was younger pot was big, too. And everybody was
getting stoned and trying it, experimenting. People kind of
got really scared of heroin. Are you saying that people
either aren't scared or they want to do it anyway?**

R: They're not scared.

R: Something to do with some of the music that's going around these days, also. Like I listen to rap 100% but I respect other kinds of music.

R: One of the guys I grew up with, [name], he died. And we went to high school and middle school. And that was the time when I was probably the most addicted to it. Just near the end. And it really didn't faze me. I didn't even think about it really. I just thought, well, he didn't know what he was doing.

R: One thing one of my friends said when one of our good friends died from a heroin overdose is that you've got to respect the drug. And I turned around and I knocked him out. Because you don't say something like that after somebody died from the drug. It has nothing to do whatsoever with respecting the drug. His point — I agree, you've got to respect the drug for what it is. But his point was that [name], my friend who died, didn't respect the drug and that's why he died. And there's a lot of that going around and that's their attitude that they're having—is people are dying because they're not giving the respect it deserves.

R: I just think since it's in the form now that you can snort it instead of shoot it up, that's probably why people are less scared of it.

They don't think they'll get addicted?

R: Well, I just don't think many people consider themselves as much of like junkies if they're not shooting it up.

R: You can shoot up speed, coke —

R: As soon as you can snort it then you feel oh, well, cool.

R: I feel like there's a loss of motivation in our generation with kids who—they just don't care anymore. You live paycheck to paycheck, you do whatever you want—and they're just not doing anything. I think that a lot of people aren't—they just don't care. I've seen a lot of people drop out of school but then they don't go do anything. People just don't care as much anymore.

Why don't they care?

R: I don't really know. I know just from—I went back to my high school to talk to a teacher and get something and they were telling me that the kids, they just don't care. And our age group, I think by our age you've sort of got your head on straight and you're figuring things out. But I just think a lot of people, they just don't care. And I don't know where it comes from or why. And that's why you get into that—some people get into a slump and just keep doing it more and more, and other people are casual users or however you do it your business—but I do think that there's a lack of motivation in a lot of things these days.

Are other people seeing it? Does it tie in?

R: I think it's about 50–50. Because I think there's always been people that don't care. And there's always been people that do. . . . In the media, the outlook on youth is that they don't care. And you're reading that and hearing that all the time. And they just ran an article recently about how—it's called the Y generation—but it focused more on what people are doing, it was a really good article. And then there's an editorial follow-up on it. And there's a lot of kids that are angry about how much bad media their generation's getting. Because if you actually go to a lot of places you can find probably more good going on than bad. Like in schools. But it's just more obvious, the bad. It's easier to focus on that.

What's the good?

R: I have a lot of friends that are still in high school. Like my friend's little sister, I'm good friends with her and she's still in high school. But all of her friends do community service, volunteer a lot. Do a lot of stuff, a lot of positive things. And that's the majority.

R: Something also popped into my head. I don't think it's more that they don't care, I think it's more a bigger rush that they're getting. I know everybody starts out on alcohol when they're 14, 15 and 16. And the people move to marijuana. I'm not saying anything's a gateway for another thing. But I've noticed with friends of mine that have been hooked on drugs, they didn't do it to spite anybody. They didn't do it because they didn't care. It was a big rush. There was something bigger and better out there and they wanted to attempt to try it.

Why do they want the bigger rush?

R: They're tired of the old rush. They want more.

R: It's greed.

R: The other thing I'm tired of is the in media that I've seen — blaming it on the parents. Because all these kids that I know that have a drug problem — they had a perfect home. They were raised correctly, they have manners. They can talk to my parents perfectly. Just regular people. I don't think it has anything to do with parents.

[Moving on to other trends]

R: Appearance nowadays. I believe men are taking care of themselves a lot better. I go to a salon and I'll get my hair colored or whatever. And as far as fashion and everything goes.

R: I always get my nails done.

Really?

R: Oh yeah.

What's going on? Are men more appearance-conscious today?

R: Yes. You see it on the news all the time. Like men going to health clubs and getting those facials and stuff. See it all the time.

But are people really doing it?

R: Definitely.

Why?

R: Just renewed my membership to 24-hour Fitness this morning.

Reason you did that?

R: Because I'm getting fat. And I have a bad knee and I need to work it out.

[Exploring motivations]

Are you going there because women are there? Is it a social thing?

R: No. Just to work out. Stay fit.

R: I play racquetball a whole bunch. Fun. Over at Bally's. Then work out while I'm not playing a game.

Is that appearance also?

R: I like to get buffed but not too buffed.

Why not?

R: I want to be able to fit through doors.

R: You'd be surprised how many women just stand there and watch you play basketball, racquetball, any kind of sport. Lift. Just walking through the gym. Be surprised how many eyes you catch looking at you.

R: I'm going to be in Hoop-It-Up this weekend. And there should be tons of women out there.

What is that?

R: Basketball tournament.

So guys will go in order to meet girls there?

R: It's not really like that but it happens. You don't go to meet women, you go to play basketball. But it happens all the time. Happens every year.

R: I think that fitness and sports — racquetball and basketball, stuff like that — [are a] continuation of what people may have played in high school or you're out at the track and you want to do something as a team. I like to play rec ball. I'll go up to the park and play a pick up game just because it keeps you active. Keeps a competitive edge. I like to keep the competitive edge in everything.

R: I like the way it keeps your metabolism.

R: It keeps you healthy—playing basketball really goes with the fitness.

When you say keeps your competitive edge you're thinking what?

R: I played college football and I can't—I've got a mindset and I'm really competitive. And if I sit out and not do anything I sort of—I'm not outgoing as much. I like to keep an edge. Above the rest.

So it kind of does a good thing for your personality?

R: Does a good thing for me, yeah, to go out and be rough and tough.

You mentioned getting your hair colored. Tell me about that.

R: It's just what everybody's doing nowadays.

R: It's trendy.

R: The barbershops are out.

R: Yes. Barbershops are out. People are going to salons. Guys. Going to salons paying 35, 40 bucks to get their hair colored and cut. Getting their nails done.

R: My dad thinks it's outrageous.

R: To have that look. To go out to meet people you want to look good. Because first impressions are everything.

[Get real life dialog]

When your dad says that's outrageous, what do you say?

R: I told my dad what I pay for a haircut and he's like, "You can come with me to the barbershop." He's eight dollars. But it's not the same. You're conforming to a style and the barbershop is still conforming to that style that was. Today's styles haircuts are different. Lot of men get their hair colored. Different shortcuts, different—some people bleach their hair. Everything.

Do they want it—it used to be people colored their hair they didn't want anybody to guess. Supposed to look natural.

R: Not anymore.

R: You see guys with blonde like right here.

R: Blonde on top. That's how I had mine.

R: Blonde on top regular color on the sides. And cut real short. Just had it kind of fixed forward.

R: Bleach the whole thing out.

What's the kind of look you felt . . . ?

R: Just the '90s look. There's not really a style. I'm not trying to look like a movie star or music performer. It's just to keep up with the age.

R: Lot of be yourself. Just dying your hair. It's not to keep up with anybody, it's you're yourself. And this is what you want to look like. And it's pretty much telling everybody if you don't like it, go away. This is who I am and if you can't accept it I don't want to talk to you.

R: People aren't conforming to this one way. There's so many different trends and styles, I don't judge — you can't judge a book by its cover. Girl sits behind me in class has 45 piercings and 50 tattoos and she is the nicest person in the world. I mean, it's just people are doing it. It's a trend. It's cool. She's got purple hair and there's nothing wrong with it.

R: Outside's just an extra bonus to what's on the inside.

R: It used to be people conformed to one way. If you were a prep you were like this. If you're a greaser you're like this. Whatever. Now it's like you can be whoever you want. And fashion is a big part—it accentuates who you are.

R: It used to be if you had it you were a freak and you were proud of being a freak. But now it's just I do it because I feel like doing it. It's not to stand out anymore.

Why bother to do it at all?

R: Self.

R: Something new. They're trying to express themselves any way they possibly can.

R: Yeah. I had my nipple pierced two years ago. And I did it just to do it. I was drunk, I admit it, and I just went and I got my nipple pierced. And it was cool. It was great. I went to jail a couple months later and had to take it out and I never put it back in. But it was just one of those things.

You went to jail not because of the [drugs mentioned earlier]?

R: No. Speeding ticket. But I couldn't get it back in. But I got that instead of a tattoo because if I wanted to take it out I could.

R: Because you have a tattoo for the rest of your life. That's something you've got to believe in.

[Picking up on an observation]

You've got earrings also. Tell me how you made that choice?

R: I just thought it looked cool.

Do you get reactions? Do people say "hey, that's cool?"

R: "Oh, that must have hurt."

R: See with me, I've had my earring since I was in tenth grade. And people that know me for years go when did you get an earring? It's not something that everyday people notice. It's just something that makes you feel good. And you know you look good with it.

How do you feel it makes you look?

R: It's unexplainable.

R: It's part of me now. I've had it so long.

R: It's a self-confidence thing.

R: Little girls do it at two and three. For a boy to do it's not right. I had both of them done when I was 14 years old. And my dad was a big hippie. Me and my brother went and had it done when I was 14 and he was 16. I didn't think it was cool, I just did it. Because I thought it was normal. My dad took me to go get it done.

Any of your parents get upset if you do stuff like that?

R: Yes.

R: My parents got real upset when I pierced my tongue.

[Personal reaction to prompt a reaction from the respondent]

Oh wow.

R: But I got it done not because everybody else had it. I got it done because I wanted to see what it felt like. Because your tongue's a muscle. Doesn't even hurt. Not as much as your ear does. Because your ear's cartilage and tissue. The needle just went through like butter. And I come home she just freaked out. "Take that out." And it was like a week before Thanksgiving. I couldn't eat.

Was that part of the fun?

R: No, not really. Because I've given her enough shit in my day.

Any new things happen in appearance, clothing, what people are wearing?

R: Oversized look for a lot of people. Jeans are getting bigger and bigger and bigger.

R: I'm getting sick of wearing those. I want to get some smaller jeans. I don't know what to get now.

R: I have a closet full of Jingos and I still like the big jeans.

R: That's what I like.

R: Can't ride a motorcycle with those things hanging off my butt.

R: You can go to the Armani and they're like 40 bucks.

R: Old Navy. Gap.

R: You can go to Sam's Club and get Tommy Hilfiger jeans, Polo, anything.

[Using an observation to probe for honest responses]

Are brand names really big? You obviously know them.

R: I wear Levi's. It doesn't matter.

R: Doesn't bother me at all.

R: I think it depends.

R: Depends on who you think you are.

R: Depends on where you're going and the occasion.

[Group control]

Slow down.

R: If you want to go and spend $100 on a pair of jeans go right ahead. I'm going to go to Sam's and get the same pair of jeans for 15 bucks. But without the name on it.

[Probing because the denial of brand importance is suspect]

Do people notice? Do they say, "Hey, it's Armani"?

R: Yes. They say, "Hey, nice jeans."

R: Like the Dockers, khaki pants — you can put on a shirt and tie with it and be dressed up. Take it right off, put on a regular shirt and go out casual. So that's all I wear. I wear jeans every once in a while.

What's the story on teen mothers, teen weddings?

R: More girls are getting pregnant at younger ages now.

R: Unprotected sex.

R: Guys don't know when to pull out.

R: Exactly.

But are they using condoms?

R: No. *[Others agree]*

R: I, for one, do. Because I hate to admit it, but I do sleep around a lot. And I was in a relationship for a year and a half and it just got old. And after I got out of that I just —just started sleeping with a lot of people.

R: One, you don't want to catch anything from anybody. Some drop-dead gorgeous female in a club, take her home with you and all of a sudden find out she has syphilis. Like ah—what?

So what are people doing about that?

R: I ask before the clothes come off. I say, "Are you protected because I know I am. So as long as you are then we're cool." But I'll still wear a condom regardless.

R: Oh, exactly.

R: Or two. It depends.

R: There you go.

R: All depends.

[Exploring a contradiction]

I'm hearing that there are a lot of pregnancies though. So obviously people aren't.

R: People just don't listen.

R: It breaks. The condom breaks. Because most teens don't know how to put it on. Especially your younger teens.

R: Lot of these pregnancies are not people in relationships.

R: One-night-stands.

R: There are mothers who they got into a relationship with some guy for one night, don't know who it was. Later on have a kid because they can't give it up or they don't want to get an abortion because of things that they've been taught.

R: Abortion's really in that underground. "Let's not talk about it." I have many friends that have gotten pregnant. And they'll get an abortion but it won't be talked about it.

R: I know four girls that are pregnant and their problem was they all got comfortable — they were in a long relationship. And I think in a lot of cases this is it. They're in a relationship where they thought they were comfortable with the guy and just decided, "Well, I don't need this protection. We've done it a million times." And they just got pregnant.

From the guys' point of view? You guys worried about it?

R: I don't want my parts falling off.

R: I'm really worried about that. I'm 21 years old. Don't have a house. I'm getting into a new career. My life would be totally ruined if I had to . . .

R: Exactly.

R: . . . down the drain. I think a lot of guys that are my age think about that. Yet when it comes down to it in the heat of the moment, it's not there. It's not in their head. That's not what they're thinking.

I'm hearing there's a lot of partying; people are drinking hard. People bar hopping.

R: It all goes together.

R: In my mind I'm more worried about myself catching a disease. But if it came down to it and I got a girl pregnant, yeah, I'd take responsibility and take care of the child. Regardless of who she is I'd take responsibility.

[This is a way to ask, do you really mean that?]

Even if you were like 19 you'd get married?

R: I wouldn't marry her but damn right I'd take care of that child.

R: I'd make her get an abortion because I'm not old enough to have kids.

R: That's the thing that everybody thinks is I can make her do this. But when it comes down to it . . .

R: You can't.

R: I'd really try to persuade her.

R: But she has the final decision.

R: Exactly.

R: That's what everybody's saying is when it happens I'll just make her get an abortion and they're not using condoms. Tons of my friends have said that. And when it comes down to it—one of my roommates—he'll sleep with any girl that'll come in his bedroom. And does he use protection? No.

What's his attitude? Doesn't matter?

R: It's "I forgot."

Abortion's easy enough to get down here?

R: Oh yeah. It's easy enough to get.

R: Planned Parenthood.

R: Any Planned Parenthood.

R: They have them in the *TV Guide*, or like the magazines you get in the paper. For abortion clinics.

R: Another thing that's really big that I just thought of — fake pregnancies.

R: To get money or clothes.

[Repeating a respondent comment]

Girls are trying to pretend they're pregnant? That's kind of from a soap opera?

R: I don't watch soap operas but [a friend's] complaining because there's three soap operas at once that had fake pregnancies on them. That like one of the characters was pretending to be pregnant.

R: My real life soap opera. My roommate's ex-girlfriend tried to get him back because she faked a pregnancy. Then she faked an abortion. She wasn't too smart about it. The procedure's supposed to be a six-hour deal. She was done in two hours and she drove herself home. And she was getting drunk that night.

R: See, she was supposed to be sedated for a while before she got to the clinic, be there for six hours and then have another person take her home and she was supposed to sleep all day.

R: And then the ultimate test was on Mother's Day. It didn't phase her a bit.

So I assume they did not go out anymore? Or did they?

R: They're still sleeping together. But that's about it.

R: Was that before or after the mandatory three-week waiting period?

R: They went five months without talking to each other.

R: Because after a girl gets an abortion she's supposed to wait three weeks before she has sex. Because . . .

R: And this is just stuff that happens every day.

What are relationships and dating like? Just kind of sleeping around?

R: Dating is cool. Relationships suck.

R: Unless you meet the right person.

R: I was tired of dating. I've been going out with the same girl for almost a year. I did the dating thing for plenty of time. And it got boring. Now I look back and it was a lot of fun. But it's like I'm in love and I'm really happy. If you're happy . . .

R: That's all that matters.

R: . . . that's all that matters, right.

R: If you find somebody and you're in love then stick with that person.

R: I was in a relationship for a year and a half with a total bitch. I mean, she was Satan. And I didn't find this out till later. But since then I started managing one of the biggest bands in Dallas now. And I meet new people every night. You just meet these people, you just start going out with them. First it might start happening, you just might hang out with them for a while, whatever. And then you just sleep together. That's the way it is. Then meet more people, sleep with them. More people, sleep with them.

So is it that you drop the one you've slept with, always going on to somebody new? Do people stay together at all?

R: You decide when you meet a person within the first ten seconds if you'd sleep with them or not.

R: But it depends. I guess nowadays [men] aren't getting a chance to — giving the women a chance to get to know them. To get to know what they're really like.

So it's kind of a series of one-night stands pretty much?

R: Pretty much.

R: Not just the guy's fault. Could be on the girl's too.

R: And the women are doing it.

R: I've seen some females just . . . like last night, me and my friend were over at Spring Valley. These two girls in a red RX-7 pulled up next to us, wanted to do something. They followed us all the way back to Plano. And I was just like . . . Well they got out, it was cool.

So did everybody get together?

R: Yes. But it wasn't on us. We were just trying to go back home. And these girls pulled up next to us.

Much more aggressive.

R: Sometimes that intimidates guys because you think about it and it's like, "Okay, if she'll sleep with me on the first night how many times is she doing this in a week?"

R: How many other people is she sleeping with?

But do people care?

R: All guys really need is a time and a place. Women it usually takes a little more.

R: Little finessing.

And your comment, dating is good but relationships suck?

R: Yeah. If you get in one for too long it just sort of wears you down. All sorts of mental games start going on.

[Use either/or question]

What do people think when they see a couple that is together? You said you've been seeing somebody. Do you find people kind of kid you about it or do they like that idea?

R: Some people are like, "Why?" And other people are like they wish they could be that way. But the people — I think the people who are saying why really wish that they could be that way. Because I wish — dating was kind of hard. It used to be hard. It used to be you had look around but now it's really easy. I was tired of it. Going and picking up girls and doing that. I found someone that I really liked and it's easy and I know. She comes home to my place every time and it's really nice.

R: I guess the reason I'm not giving women a chance nowadays to get to know them is because most of them are gold diggers. If you don't have a good job and a nice automobile, they won't give you the time of day. But if you do then you know, they'll stay with you for a while. As long as you keep them happy.

R: That's something I run into a lot because my roommate works at [a] bar. And I go to [name] Pub all the time. And I run into a lot of females that I hit on and maybe go out with once or twice. And then when they realize that I have no money, that I get a lot of drinks for free in all these bars and that's why I can get them all their drinks. And then they come back to my house and they see I live in a nice house and they find out I don't have money. "Talk to you later. Bye. Nice knowing you."

R: I'm not in that area. I have a girlfriend—she and I don't sleep together — we kind of stated together that we would remain virgins until we got married. And that became an option to get married.

[Despite all the talk about sex, this respondent had the guts to say he's still a virgin]

R: That's real good. I said that when I was a kid. And I said I wanted to do that.

R: Well, I still sleep around but I'm still a virgin. I just don't have actual intercourse.

[One of the other men bragging about his sex life now admits he's more innocent too]

Why is it important to you to stay a virgin?

R: I just haven't met the right person yet. I just haven't found that person I care enough about. And one of my best friends put it in words I could never put it in. Ten years down the line I'll look back, no matter if it's a one-night stand or a long relationship, I want to be able to say I don't regret giving that gift to that person. And I haven't found that person yet that I can look 10, 20, 30 years down the line no matter where I'm at in life and say, "Man, I shouldn't have done that. I wish I'd waited or I wish I'd found the right person."

R: I agree with that. I don't want to regret it. Regret I didn't wait till my wedding night.

Is that a religious thing?

R: Yeah, it's kind of religious. I go to church and everything. Not only that. Just a personal goal I've kind of set for myself.

[Call on a quiet respondent]

Zack, want to comment on relationships?

R: I try and get out of them. That's the only problem I have. Once I'm in them—because I don't like saying this isn't going to work out. Because there's some crazy, crazy women out there.

_____ ***And then what happened?***

What did *Playboy* do with the research when it was done? Of course, the focus groups provided ideas for the quantitative survey among a nationally representative sample of men, helping them to write a thought-provoking questionnaire that not only quantified what we had heard, but was also designed to yield newsworthy results.

The videotapes were edited down to create a montage of men's attitudes in the 1990s as a "road show" for advertisers. This gave them the opportunity to let them in on the insights we gained from the guys we spoke with. And it has served as a springboard for further research across a variety of product and demographic categories.

CHAPTER 10

The Moderator as Trend Detective

Qualitative research is "small-scale" but it reveals the "big picture" too

IN THE 21ST CENTURY, the rate of change keeps speeding up, making it more important than ever for marketers to stay current with consumers' lifestyles. They need to know what people care about and how they are living so they can create products, services, and advertising that are relevant and effective. Focus groups and other qualitative research methods are increasingly helping marketers track important trends. Large-scale surveys of the public, both in the United States and internationally, are indispensable, of course, in providing information about trends. Some have years of data so they can benchmark trends over the years.

When I first started conducting focus groups in the early 1970s, qualitative research often was not thought of as a way to detect and understand trends. Almost by definition, qualitative research entails using small-scale samples that may not be projectable and it purposely uses non-standardized questions. That is its strength and, at the same time, the reason why marketers and researchers typically have thought of qualitative research as appropriate mainly for "generating" hypotheses for larger studies.

The projects I worked on at the beginning of my career were on very specific, narrow marketing issues (vitamins, household cleaners, upset stomach remedies, wigs, etc.). I trotted home and told my friends what fascinating things I was hearing about what people outside New York were thinking and doing. My god, there was a feminist revolution taking place! Homemakers in Midwestern suburbs were declaring they cared more about being "a real person" than having a spotless home. Often they started by stating, "I'm not a feminist but. . ." and then said they believed women should receive pay equal to men's. It became apparent that I wasn't just doing a series of individual studies; I was gaining a broad-ranging picture of Americans' lives at a time of tremendous change. In addition to product-focused studies, my work over the last two decades has also included broad-ranging lifestyle studies of demographic groups and different areas of life — the "mature" market, health and fitness, etc.

Like a number of other qualitative researchers, I may speak to about 2,000 people around the U.S. in the course of a single year. These are firsthand interviews where I see or at least hear what people have to say in their own words. Having done qualitative research for a long time, I have an informal longitudinal view of consumers and business people, too — how they have changed over time and, equally important, how they have not changed. These interviews add up. Themes cut across studies; the same types of people (women, teenagers, baby boomers, etc.) are interviewed on many different studies. I'm not saying that these all add up to quantitative research; if you're interested in numbers, do a statistical study. However, a larger picture does emerge.

Patterns of thought and behavior I have seen repeatedly in my research can be a surprise to clients

Over the years, I've found that patterns of thought and behavior I have seen repeatedly in my research can be a surprise to clients who observe just a few focus groups. My clients will often have a picture in their minds of different groups of people — Gen Xers as all looking "grungy," or of affluent people all dripping in gold jewelry, for example — that don't match up with reality.

Qualitative research provides a great way to:

Identify new, emerging patterns. At first, there are probably just a few respondents making comments that we realize we haven't heard before. For example, the way respondents introduce themselves can signal possible demographic shifts. Adults (especially women) may say they are returning to school to further or change careers. "Semi-retired" people may have officially retired from their jobs but continue to work on a part-time basis, serve as consultants, or do work for fun. Moonlighting entrepreneurs may talk about working full-time while they start a business on the side. "Single parent" is a proud new label that replaced specific descriptions like divorced or not married — it presumes that how/why that person became a single parent is none of your business. "Stay-at-home-mom" seems to have replaced "housewife" and "home-maker," showing women are emphasizing their role as parents, not their ties to the home. It's commonplace today to hear people describe themselves as gay, that they live with a "significant other," or have children from several marriages in the household. Sometimes the people we have difficulty locating provide a lesson in shifting

> QUALITATIVE RESEARCH
>
> ▶ *Identify new, emerging patterns*
> ▶ *Understand existing trends*
> ▶ *Discover the future*
> ▶ *Observe counter-trends*

demographics. We're unable to recruit full-time home-makers who do not plan to return to paid employment, married women aged 50 and older who are not involved in their family's financial decision-making, or a full group of people aged 40 and older who have been married for 20 or more years.

Understand existing trends. What are the motivations behind current trends? How do people feel about and experience current trends? When the health trend was growing in the 1980s, for instance, the depth of feeling consumers had about the benefits (looking better, feeling better, the hope of living longer) convinced some clients that this was not a passing fad. At the same time, the resistance many people had to giving up "goodies" suggested that there was an opportunity for guilt-free "naughty" products as well as flat-out "sinful" ones. In its quest for novelty, the media often overlook the continuation of a trend. "Smart shopper" bargain-seeking hit a peak in the 1990s during the recession. The economy has improved, with millions of people benefiting from the stock-market boom. However, we still hear consumers and business people tell us that they look for good prices and love the "thrill" of great buys. If anything, the Internet has encouraged and facilitated bargain seeking. It's an apparent contradiction, but smart shopping has simply become a habit for many consumers. The same person who will splurge on an expensive dinner or new outfit may also brag about finding a terrific deal. Moreover, keep in mind that not everyone has benefited from the nation's overall economic improvement.

Signposts for the future. When people are excited about something, when they attempt to persuade others to try

When people are excited about something, when they attempt to persuade others to try something, what they show off about, and what they get riled up about are all indications of dynamic movement

something, what they show off about, and what they get riled up about are all indications of dynamic movement in the consumer psyche. A respondent raves about how great the Internet is for researching travel and everyone else immediately asks for and writes down the name of the website. This demonstrates the growing interest in using the Internet for trip information. Conversely, when even Internet-savvy people shake their heads fiercely, stating they do not want to use their credit cards to shop online, this shows that resistance is still strong. There are times when we can see that current attitudes are open to future change. In the 1998 Mantrack study for *Playboy*, privacy of computerized personal information didn't spark any strong emotions. Even when I probed for respondents' feelings about companies and the government knowing what they read, buy, watch, and so on, they expressed indifference. "The only real area of concern," our report said, "seemed to be the stealing of credit-card numbers."

Going further, we speculated: "The fact that privacy drew fairly indifferent reactions does not mean that it might not be an issue, however. Specific cases might raise it to headline status. If the public feels that the case represents an injustice and, perhaps more to the point, if they feel 'it could happen to me,' there might be greater concern."

Trends may also fade. In our consumer and business research, we don't hear environmental concerns come up often compared with the 1990s, for instance. If we were to ask directly about respondents' concern with the environment, a number might say this is "important," but the fact that the subject comes up with less spontaneous frequency gives me an indication that some con-

Sometimes we can see that current attitudes are open to future change

sumers feel less passionately about the issue than they once did.

Observe counter–trends. For every trend, there is a counter-trend, often unnoticed by the media. In this counter-trend may be a larger trend emerging for the future. Right now, the Internet is hot, of course. While an increasing number of people are using it for news, research, and entertainment, we're also hearing a number of people say they do not want to log on at home. After days spent largely on a computer at work, they prefer to read, watch television, or talk to their families. Cell phones are another example. Usage has surged for a variety of practical and status reasons—and so has a backlash as more people complain of the dangers while driving, and the rudeness and intrusiveness of others' conversations. It seems a good bet that cell-phone ownership and use will continue to rise because this tool is now an established part of people's personal and business lives, but that the backlash will be its companion. Media's depiction of the jerk-on-the-phone is likely to be a staple, especially of comedy.

Trends and counter- trends often co-exist

Trends and counter-trends can co-exist. On the one side, many Americans now take it for granted that traditional values have changed. Even if they are living a "traditional" life themselves, they are no longer shocked that other people are not. In a focus group a few years ago in Philadelphia, a city once known for its conservatism, a respondent in an all-female group casually mentioned that she has an infant and that she and her boyfriend like going out to the clubs. No one looked surprised in the least. On the other side, respondents in many groups talk about the decline in moral values, referring not just to sexuality and family. The same people sometimes at once espouse and condemn their own values. They are disapproving, for instance, of rampant materialism, saying their parents were more concerned with saving for the future than with amassing "goodies." Yet, they admit they love to live well and have no intention of changing. What does this apparent muddle mean? It opens the potential to appeal to both segments and both sides.

Trend traps

There are several traps in trend spotting. Good qualitative research can help bring us back to reality by getting beyond the buzzwords to see how people are really living.

The exaggeration trap. Forecasters and marketers often like simplicity, confidently stating that this is the big trend, where everything's headed. For example, everyone's cocooning — withdrawing to their homes rather than going out; everyone's on the Internet and the "offline" world is disappearing, and so on. While we need to look at growth areas, it's usually misleading to simply pronounce that the world is moving in just one direction. Basic human needs remain — most people are social creatures who seek connections, whether online or in-person; most people want to get out of the house some of the time. The forms of our behavior change but many needs stay the same.

Looking back on trend pronouncements that didn't pan out, one in the 1970s was that we would soon be living in a unisex world, where gender differences would not matter or be noticeable. Certainly, a dramatic shift in gender roles was very apparent in the focus groups I was moderating at that time. Many women moved into higher-level positions in the workplace. It became more acceptable for mothers of young children to be employed. Muscular, strong bodies for women started to look not just okay, but sexy. On the male side, men were expressing their feelings more openly, dressing in more relaxed and sometimes flamboyant ways, and getting more involved in parenting, as it became more accept-able to be "sensitive" rather than macho. However, it was naïve to think that old gender roles had disappeared.

One trend pronouncement of the 1970s that didn't pan out was that we would soon be living in a unisex world

Over the last few decades, there has been zigzagging of gender roles on both sides. Some of the changes have become integrated in American life. Today's fathers are far more involved with their children than their own fathers were, taking on the chores as well as the fun stuff — but many are still less involved than the mothers would like. While sex before marriage is taken for granted by many young people, so are the old rules in dating: the man makes the first move, he pays for the first date, etc. While many women are in the workplace and many run their own businesses, many also choose to stay home full-time for several years to be with young children. Greater communication exists, but the battle of the sexes continues. Both men and women make dis-paraging remarks about the other sex along conventional lines — women just love to shop, men are just big babies under their façade,

TREND TRAPS

The exaggeration trap
Forecasters and marketers often like simplicity, confidently stating that this is the big trend, where everything's headed

The logic trap
Many forecasts turn out to be wrong because they assume people act rationally

The static trap
Trend spotters may overlook the fact that situations are dynamic, that parties respond to new circumstances

The trendy trend trap
Long-term trends often start out looking like short-term fads, but many short-term fads never become long-term trends

and so on. Underlying this zigzagging, I believe, is the tension that not only exists between the sexes but within many individuals as well. The battles that divided American society in the 1960s continue: respect for parental and governmental authority, gender roles, sexuality, and race. Expect more in the future.

Many forecasts turn out to be wrong because habit/inertia and emotions are far more powerful than logic

The logic trap. Many forecasts turn out to be wrong because they assume people act rationally. Habit/inertia and emotions, however, are often far more powerful than logic. In television programming, for example, there's still the idea of "lead-in"— that programs can benefit from a strong preceding program. Logic would seem to dictate that the advent of the remote control, where anyone can easily switch channels with the flick of a finger, would have killed the "lead-in" concept, but it hasn't. The continued importance of the "lead-in" may reflect not only laziness but also a sense of connection to a particular network. Digital watches and clocks were predicted to replace the "old-fashioned" analog ones, but they didn't. Instead, the ones with hands fit the way many people think. It's a quarter of ten, not 9:45; and the ones with hands look nicer.

The static trap. Forecasts often fail to take into account that situations are dynamic. As the Internet grows, physical stores and shopping centers will work harder to attract customers. As childbirth outside of marriage increases, conservatives will work harder to discourage these pregnancies.

The trendy trend trap. Long-term trends often start out looking like short-term fads but many short-term fads never become long-term trends. Fads can make a huge amount of money for a while, of course. The danger is they can quickly fizzle out, leaving manufacturers and retailers with far too many bell-bottom pants. A good deal of trend spotting focuses on trendsetters: the forerunners and early adopters who are usually the first to try new things. Teenagers, urban ethnic youth, and the affluent are among the trendsetters worth following. Sometimes mainstream people copy these new products and styles, but other times the fad goes no further. Trendsetters are often motivated, whether they admit it or not, by the quest for novelty and attention. Once something has become mainstream, the trendies will often reject it and move on in their search for the next novelty, product, fashion, or experience.

Most of my research focuses on mainstream people. They do not seek out newness for newness's sake; in fact, a number prefer to wait until they feel something has been tested and is widespread enough to avoid attracting attention. They didn't want to walk down the street or sit by the hotel pool yakking on a cell phone when no one else was. However, many have bought one now that cell phones are relatively standard and can be justified in practical terms. Women in our research talk about the safety benefit of a cell phone: it takes some of the fear out of driving alone at night. (Of course, once you have it, you end up using it to order Chinese food, but that's another story.) Back in the 1980s, when mainstream people began saying that a VCR was a good idea because teenagers would stay home and the entire family would watch a movie together, it was obvious that this technology had established itself.

Fads that are more likely to become long-term trends satisfy people's deeper needs

Fads are fickle. They are hard, if not impossible, to forecast.

Speculating on which new patterns may become trends is less subject to fashion. Those that are more likely to stick around satisfy people's deeper needs, have multiple reasons for being, and tie into broader demographic and economic trends. The health and fitness trend, for instance, connects with fear of death, the aging of the population, the desire to look good and have a positive self-image. Eating chicken and fish makes people feel they are watching their health, their weight, and saving money — a great combination of motives. Similarly, the counter-trend to drink, smoke, and eat fatty foods ties in with what I call the need to be naughty, the long-term trend of stressed-out lives and, in some cases, youth. Fads are most likely to become trends when they are anchored to deep needs.

Deep needs that anchor trends include:

- Safety (physical and psychological)
- Economic stability
- Positive self image, self worth
- Social connection with family, friends, the workplace, community, and religion
- Power and influence over one's world
- The quest for longer life, immortality

Major trends

TREND: *Time trade-offs*

Once upon a time, futurists predicted that the biggest problem we would face in the 21st century was finding something to do to fill our empty days. Technology would be doing all the work, after all. Somehow it didn't work out that way. Remember the paperless office? Or how much time that cell phone and that ATM were going to create for you? What happened to it all?

While researchers today may still debate whether we're actually busier today than we were several decades ago, there's no doubt in the mind of consumers: we feel time crunched. "I need a wife!" has been the standard cliché for women over the last 15 years.

So should you speed it up, streamline it, or make it go faster if you're providing a product or service to the public? Should you forget reading, forget shopping in a store if it all takes too long? Not necessarily. Every trend has its counterbalance, and this one is reveling in the luxury of downtime, to take the time to do something as unhurried as browsing in a store or reading a book. There are opportunities in both fast and slow gear.

The clear message from consumers is that it's okay for me to take my time, but it's not okay for you to waste my time. Even when the time crunch is intense, it is also naïve to take lack of time as the real reason why people do or don't do something. Time has become the all-purpose excuse today. Often, there's more beneath the surface. Subscribers stop getting a magazine because they don't have time to read it — but they usually switch to another one. People don't floss their teeth — but it only takes a minute. Usually something else is going on too. The magazine no longer interests them, requires too much concentration, or they're "brain dead" after work. Flossing is uncomfortable or they don't know how to do it properly.

MAJOR TRENDS
▶ *Time trade-offs*
▶ *In on the game*
▶ *Complementarity*
▶ *Generational power*
▶ *Who's got the money?*
▶ *Nostalgia*
▶ *Confident woman*
▶ *Flexible lifestages*
▶ *Zigzagging women*
▶ *Zigzagging men*
▶ *Common ground between the sexes*
▶ *Not the old 9-to-5*
▶ *Travel as an American right*
▶ *Community-seeking*

TREND: *In on the game*

Consumers know that they're being pitched to, which adds a whole layer of complexity to marketing. This is a relatively new phenomenon. About five years ago, I started hearing respondents talk about positioning and asking who is the target audience for the product.

Just because they know it's marketing doesn't mean that they're turned off. In fact, there's a real difference today in consumer attitudes towards marketing and advertising. When I was doing research in the 1970s, I'd hear many people talk about how they hated advertising. Now most people accept it. If you're not treating them like idiots, people don't mind if you're selling to them. In fact, a lot of people like advertisements, if they're done well.

That's not to say that the backlash to commercialism is entirely dead. I recently saw a T-shirt in the window of an athletic footwear store that proudly pronounced, "endorsed by nobody." At present, this backlash isn't strong, but it may well grow.

The clear message from consumers: it's okay for me to take my time, but it's not okay for you to waste my time

If consumers are more aware today, they can also be surprisingly trusting. Some might even be called naïve savants. They may say, on a general level, that the Internet has a lot of "garbage" information, yet believe what they see. In a study of automotive shopping, for instance, we found that people who did online research took the information at face value. They tended to ignore the company behind a website. On company X's website, the statement that its vehicle is superior to others was not questioned despite its obviously self-interested source.

TREND: *Complementarity*

Despite the many predictions and hype about the Internet taking over, a growing trend is the complementary roles the online and real worlds are playing. Yes, indeed, more people are using the Internet than ever; as they discover its many practical and entertaining uses, more people will use it more often in the future. This doesn't mean that "old" forms are disappearing, however. Many people still want to shop at "real" stores or read "hard copy" books and magazines rather than squint at a computer screen, especially after working at a computer all day. As a result, there have been more and more crossovers. Established companies are getting online and, although some swore they would never do it, online companies are opening stores, launching magazines, and so on. The reality is that consumers and businesses see a need for both. Print and broadcast media serve a scanning purpose; the Internet is for searching. Print and broadcast ads create brand awareness for a website, then people go online. Online shopping can be done any time, "going" to sources all over the world; store shopping lets people touch and try on merchandise and can be social.

Many people still want to shop at "real" stores or read "hard copy" books and magazines rather than squint at a computer screen

TREND: *Generational power*

The baby boomers have been a marketers' delight since their birth because of the huge size of their group and, later, because of their willingness to spend. Now that they are "aging," with early boomers in their 50s, some marketers are developing products and media for this generation which refuses to consider itself old ("youthening" fashion and beauty, "active" rather than "retirement" communities, movies like "Space Cowboys" about old codgers who outwit the young guys). The counter-trend is represented by marketers who have lost interest in the boomers whom they call "over-the-hill," switching their attention from the crowd to the next big demographic bulge, Generation Y. Fears that Social Security will run out are likely to ignite some generational battles over issues like retirement age. The result of all this may well be that Generation X, relatively small compared to its two bookends, may be the most ignored.

TREND: *The American Dream*

The way in which the American Dream is expressed undergoes change

People's goals and, indeed, things they feel entitled to include: believing that each generation should do better in income and status than the previous one, owning one's own home, having at least one vehicle, owning one's own business, being an entrepreneur, taking vacation trips. The way in which the dream is expressed undergoes change. Home ownership, for instance, is now the goal of single men and women starting in their 20's, rather than being delayed until marriage. Home-buying rates vary, of course, but the desire remains, which means that when economic conditions are favorable, they increase again. Entrepreneurs may be mothers working from home or dot-com twentysomethings whose company just went public. Increasingly, people say, "You have to make your own security," that owning a business is less risky than working for a big corporation which has no loyalty to its workers. Vacations are viewed as important to one's psychological well-being; taking the kids to a Disney park is almost a parental duty. Inability to achieve these goals can make people feel deprived, especially middle class ones who grew up assuming they would be able to do so.

TREND: *Money, money, who's got the money?*

Americans' love of success, defined by many in financial terms, seems to come and go with the country's economic well-being. When the economy is doing well, more open displays of consumption are welcomed. The status symbols may change — after all, one of the benefits of wealth is doing what's new. If it was a Cadillac in the 1950s, now it's an SUV. Certain old symbols remain vital or return to favor —the Rolls Royce, antique furniture, diamonds. Role models are people who have attained their success in whatever is the best contemporary route, whether corporate, entrepreneurial, or artistic. When times are bad, though, it becomes more popular to mock the rich in media, to denounce money-grubbing.

TREND: *Nostalgia*

Nostalgia is a trend that's here to stay. For many of us, childhood is a period that we romanticize. This was not always the case. People who grew up during the Great Depression were less nostalgic about their childhood than people who grew up in more comfortable times. Moreover, it's hard to imagine that the 1980s will ever have a comeback like the 1960s has experienced.

Our outlooks and perceptions are linked to relative prosperity more than most of us would like to admit

One reason why boomers are nostalgic for the 1950s is that it was a time of prosperity when families stayed together, like it or not. Although many would not want to return to this confined lifestyle, they wistfully remember it as "simpler." The music and the stars of that period continue to have great vitality, not just with boomers but with their children as well. Ironically, this nostalgia makes boomers feel youthful, although their tenacity in hanging onto it reflects, at least in part, their fear of aging. GenXers and GenYs, born after the 1960s, are nostalgic for the 1950s, too, as a symbol of freedom and fun. In time, of course, these younger generations will be nostalgic for their own "good old days."

It seems likely that the late 1990s, the era of the bull market, will also have its comeback in the future. And, looking ahead, the generation that grew up in economic good times will probably be nostalgic for its childhood.

TREND: *I am woman: I am confident*

When I started doing qualitative research in the early 1970s, I mainly interviewed "housewives"—a term that is deservedly out of favor now, women don't marry their house—rather than employed women, a small and ignored segment.

These homemakers often put themselves down, describing themselves by saying "I'm just a housewife." When a product didn't work, they blamed themselves. There was a lot of guilt. A big cliché in those days had housewives cooped up in the house all day wanting to get out, but they felt guilty when they admitted that they had needs outside the family.

By the mid-to-late 1970s, this started to change. By the 1980s, it had really changed. Women still have a bit of a guilt hangover from their days as expected homebodies, and some of the old expectations about being "taken care of" by a man certainly still exist. These things are not simple, and they are more like a pendulum swinging than a complete transformation, but the trend is clear: women are much more confident.

In the 1970s, many women were not aware of their own finances or did not even know their family income. Today, many women are financially independent. If they are married, they take an active role in money management, whether or not they are currently earning an income. They buy many products once targeted just at men: cars, homes, and fine jewelry. Many successfully invest their own money. Because those roles are relatively new—even for younger women—there is a sense of pride, a thrill in mastery.

In the 1970s, many women did not even know their family income; today, many women are financially independent

At the same time, many women find financial management boring and confusing. Some want to know more, and unlike their male counterparts, honestly admit their ignorance. Others prefer to depend on their husbands or financial professionals for help.

TREND: *Flexible lifestages*

The life schedule people were expected to follow in the 1950s was clear: get married following school (high school or college); have children starting in your 20s; if you are a woman, stop working once you have children; become an empty nester in your 40s; retire in your 60s. Nowadays, this "predictable" life cycle seems scrambled. Imagine a room with four 38-year-old women: One has never had children; one just had her first child; another has a child in college; and the other is a grandmother. One stays home full-time; one works part-time; one works full-time and owns her own business; and one has returned to school for further education. One is married for the second time; one is living with her "significant other;" one is a single mother; and the fourth is unattached to either children or a spouse. Most surprising, not one of these women is especially unusual. They experience a sense of freedom to live their own lives on their own schedule. If this sounds obvious to you, think of a client's request for a proposal which asks for singles in their 20s, married people in their 30s, empty nesters over age 45, and retired people over age 55. The stereotyping has, unfortunately, outlived the reality.

Today the "predictable" life cycle seems scrambled

TREND: *Zigzagging women*

Does this greater diversity mean that all the old pressures on women are gone? No. Women are more confident but the "shoulds" remain and they are stronger in the more conservative areas of the country. The pressures come from society, family, and internally. In fact, because the rules have loosened, it can be more confusing deciding what's the right thing to do. The dilemma of choice replaces no (real) choice. Mothers of young children still worry about making the right choice between staying home and getting a job outside the home that may entail day care. Today there are more options — paid work; running a business from home; working part-time — but it's still a tough decision. On both sides of the stay-home decision, many women feel torn and criticized. Homemakers are such a minority that they worry about being viewed as women who "just watch soap operas and eat bon-bons" rather than bringing in income and developing their work talents. Women without children often debate whether to have a child. Again, there are more choices — to have a child as a single woman with or without a male or female partner, to adopt, to go the route of surrogate birth, and so forth. They debate what's best for them personally and, of course, for the child.

The dilemma of choice replaces no (real) choice

Another way in which roles for women have zigzagged is in being a "sex object." During the 1960s revolution, feminists resented this highly confining role. As many women moved into career positions, they were advised to play down their sexuality to be taken seriously — wear the "uniform" of a suit with the female version of a tie, exchange the pocketbook for a briefcase, and so on. Now, it seems, many women want to express their "femininity" in their dress. Tied in with the casualization trend, many wear tight-and-slight outfits that draw attention to their bodies. There's the 21st century twist as women over 50 (years) and over 150 (pounds) go to work wearing midriff-bearing sleeveless tops with bra straps peeking through.

The message: "I feel great!" My guess is that the next move will be away from these outfits, both because fashion seeks change and because some women will feel uncomfortable with the attention they receive.

With the aging of the population, we can expect to see more role models of "growing old gracefully"— women who look great after age 40. Think about Rene Russo, Jane Seymour, Jane Fonda, Goldie Hawn, and Cher. Does this mean that American women have stopped worrying about lines and wrinkles? I only wish.

TREND: *Zigzagging men*

Men have their own zigzag, because the messages that they've been sent by society have been so schizophrenic. Are men supposed to be Mister Macho, always non-expressive and the reliable breadwinner? (Think Arnold Schwarzenegger.) Or are they supposed to be sensitive and caring? (Think Alan Alda.) As female roles have changed, it's inevitable that they would also have an impact on male roles. The fact is that for both genders, we're still not quite sure whether we're ready — or even want — to shed all vestiges of our former traditional roles.

In terms of dress, men have experienced their own liberation of late. It used to be that professional men had to wear a suit and tie, but the casual late 1990s has relieved men in most professions of the need to be that formal — and, let's face it, boring. Men have more opportunities than ever before to be self-expressive in their clothing. It should be noted that African-American men were there long before it moved out to the white male culture. Still, a limiting factor in wardrobe decisions is something that has not changed for many heterosexual men. They are still afraid of looking like they are gay. (Women, on the other hand,

The fact is that for both genders, we're still not quite sure whether we're ready—or even want—to shed all vestiges of our former traditional roles

do not seem to worry about being viewed as lesbian.)

When I did the Mantrack study for *Playboy*, I found that the "bad boy" syndrome was alive and well. It's a backlash against the "feminization" of men—the "boys will be boys" idea. This is perfectly embodied on Comedy Central's late-night testosterone fest, *The Man Show*. Although some men will act out in this way and lose all restraint — burping when they feel like it, scratching themselves wherever and whenever, sleeping with lots of women — the appeal of being a bad boy is mostly on a fantasy level. It's hard to give up the "fun" part of old acceptable gender roles.

The reality of men's lives is usually different. Many men are deeply involved with and committed to their families. They speak movingly and openly about their love of their wife and children. The change for men is that it is now acceptable not only to live such "traditional" lives, but to also show their need for this connection.

The appeal of being a "bad boy" is mostly on a fantasy level

© Creators Syndicate. By permission of Mike Luckovich and Creators Syndicate inc.

TREND: *Common ground between the sexes*

Although confusion over roles still exists, there is more communication in male-female relationships. The truth today is that men and women have a lot in common. It used to be that husbands went out to work and wives stayed home and their daily lives did not have that much in common. Today, with dual-income households, most couples have daily lives that contain similar experiences.

TREND: *Not the old 9-to-5*

The rise in the home office has gotten a lot of press hype. Although there is no doubt more people are working at home, I think predictions about everything moving in that direction go too far. People still need to interact. Many who work at home find it lonely — the workplace is an important social network similar to another family, an attitude we see glorified on television — and many people will never want to give up that camaraderie. They want to feel like a part of the company mission, and it's hard to inspire those feelings when everyone works in separate places.

In a society where there are fewer points of security, when our marriage or parents' marriage is not withstanding the test of time, and families are scattered throughout the country, we look for other safe harbors. That same feeling applies to the workplace.

Career, not just job, switching has become commonplace, even respected

Career, not just job, switching has become commonplace, even respected. It's not unusual to speak to a 29-year-old who is on her third career, without concern about a job-hopping resume being a drawback. You will find 45-year-olds who have quit their jobs to start a business in a new field. In fact, it's reached the point where people who stay with the same job for 30 years are considered decidedly old-fashioned and passive. If the career doesn't fit, don't keep wearing it. Some of this switching, of course, has come out of necessity as workers were downsized; now they feel that if employers have no loyalty to them, they owe no loyalty back.

The scope of work has greatly expanded for many people, contributing to the time famine. Many people are working longer hours because of leaner companies, secretary-less offices, at-home businesses without strict office hours, and more global connections at all hours. Further, many professionals feel that to stay current, they must understand what's going on in a broader world. Beyond their own job, they have to know the latest technological tools, what their company is doing overall, what's happening in their industry, trends in the United States and internationally. One consequence is the demand to keep up with the media—the Internet, the ever-growing number of trade publications, and so on. The job never seems to end.

Retirement often means continued work productivity "as I like it"

Redefined retirement is another trend we often see in other research. Certainly many people would love to retire as early as possible, a dream few achieve. What is changing is that a growing number of people at or near conventional retirement age have no intention of stopping work altogether. Some choose "semi-retirement," meaning that they work fewer hours. Others go full force into new careers or businesses. Others quit their jobs and then become consultants for the same company. Still others just keep doing what they've been doing for years. And, finally, there are those who do unsalaried work as volunteers, mentors, or investors. What all these continued workers have in common is that they have taken control of their work lives. They work because they want to, structuring their hours for greater freedom. They seek meaning and achievement in their work. The idea of "complete retirement" with unending leisure horrifies them. Looking ahead, we expect more boomers to be productive workers well into their 60s, 70s, 80s — yes, even their 90s.

TREND: *Travel as an American right*

Today, many Americans feel like they really deserve to travel and take vacations. Travel is enormously important, for a whole variety of reasons, perhaps most importantly for escape from the everyday. It's a time to bond with family and a life partner. "I think you need to travel as much as you can. Go out there and enjoy yourself," a man declared in a recent focus group. A huge amount of money goes towards travel; fantasies are built around it. Don't pay any attention to predictions that virtual reality will eliminate the need for leisure travel.

There are many different types of travelers: those who do the same thing every year; those who travel mainly with the family; those who are sophisticated and looking for new things to do. Adventure travel is a response to boredom with everyday life and the desire to feel something. People who are in good physical shape want to experience rigorous activities and to test themselves.

Children influence travel choices for their families, of course. Parents may pick a place like Disney World because it's hard to keep kids entertained all the time. Disney World does that for them. It's packaged and it's safe.

Travelers aged 50 and older are important because they have the money and, after retirement, the time to do some serious traveling. Elderhostel is interesting, although when I hear that term, I cringe. Baby boomers are not going to want to identify themselves with "Elder" anything. The American Society of Retired Persons changed its name to

Today, people feel they really deserve to travel for new experiences and as an escape from the everyday

the acronym, AARP, since many people past 50 are not retired.

There's interest in travel within the U.S. to understand different aspects of our country and one's own heritage. This ties into the nostalgia trend. I wouldn't be surprised if we had more family reunions because desire for connection is very strong today. The Internet may spawn more international travel, as people meet people from other countries online and arrange visits.

Another travel trend is the growth of the mini-vacation. This is related to the time crunch. It is easier to get away for a long weekend than a two-week vacation. The Internet helps people make spontaneous decisions and sometimes even find a travel bargain. Frequent-flier points, freebie trips, are naturally always of interest.

TREND: *Community-seeking*

It has become a truism that niche marketing has replaced mass marketing. Consumers want to be recognized as having more specialized needs, rather than being part of some amorphous gigantic market. Don't send me messages aimed at parents if I don't have kids; don't talk me to me as a corporate type if I own my own business. The Internet caters to and has increased the desire to be part of a community. Whatever one's characteristics or problems, somewhere there's probably a web site or newsgroup that's for you. The counter-trend is the great yearning people have to be part of something larger, whether on a serious or superficial level. Water cooler conversation seems to be needed as much or more than ever. People who barely know one another can talk about the Oscars ("Can you believe what she wore?"), the Super Bowl (the ads), *Who*

Consumers want to be recognized as having more specialized needs

Wants to be a Millionaire ("Is that your final answer?"), *Survivor* ("He never should have won."). While there is no easy way to predict what will capture the public's interest, the search for community means that big pop-culture hits will continue to come and go.

CHAPTER 11

15 Myths about Qualitative Research

It's conventional, but is it wisdom? _____

Certain views about the way in which qualitative research should be conducted have attained the status of conventional wisdom. But my experience suggests that these "truisms" are either not true or are not the only "right" way to do qualitative research.

Myth 1

Focus groups should never have more than six or seven respondents, so each one gets more "air time."

REALITY: The ideal number of respondents depends on the type of respondents, the subject, and the moderator's style. Most consumer focus groups we conduct have 8 to 10 respondents. The smaller the group, the lower the odds of good chemistry, which sometimes results in less energy.

However, mini-focus groups of four to six respondents have their place. Examples include groups of executives, who are highly opinionated and sometimes self-important; and teenagers, who can be very shy or, conversely, hard to control. Small groups can work well for detailed probes of decision-making and in some cases, to explore reactions to advertising.

Myth 2

Qualitative researchers should approach each study with a "clean slate" mentally. Past research by other companies, information about the clients' hunches, or internal political battles concerning the current study will only bias the researcher.

REALITY: Background on a project's real objectives and past learning is an important part of the moderator briefing. Certainly, the information could bias a moderator, but a good researcher needs to know what to look for. The moderator can probe responses that do not fit hypotheses, touching more briefly on what confirms well-accepted knowledge.

Briefing should include the product or service's contents, how it works, what it does, how it is or is not different from the competition, its history, and so on.

Often clients say, "Ask respondents what their perceptions of X are." In the focus groups, moderators should, of course, first probe for respondents' perceptions unaided. But if respondents are unaware or confused, the moderator can raise issues for them to consider. For example, "What if you knew that X is . . . ?"

Myth 3

Lots of good ideas die in focus groups because consumers are not ready to accept new concepts.

REALITY: Qualitative research offers researchers the opportunity to probe what underlies consumers' reactions. If an idea meets immediate respondent rejection, a good researcher explores the reasons why, whether the product might fit a real need and what, if anything, could change respondents' minds. Do the respondents lack knowledge? Are they anxious about newness or rejecting specific features? Is there a deeper resistance? The moderator can explore respondents' reactions when given additional information or after learning of advantages they haven't yet seen. The moderator can also explore potential changes in the product or service or in the communication.

With respect to the once-radical idea of ATMs, other bank research our firm was conducting at the time these were introduced showed that customers were frustrated by not being able to "get my money" outside regular bank hours. This suggests that the machines did correct a common problem, that a real need existed, and that there might be ways of dealing with consumer resistance.

Myth 4

Focus groups should be homogeneous demographically. Respondents should be the same gender, in the same age and income group, and so on.

REALITY: Not necessarily. Most research budgets do not afford the luxury of focus groups that differ demographically, with one group per type in each market. Some diversity can, in fact, be beneficial.

The rule of thumb is simple. Respondents must feel comfortable talking with one another about the subject. For example, children and teen-aged respondents should be in only one or two grades, and boys and girls should be kept separate.

With adults, though, successful focus groups have included both men and women together discussing consumer and business issues, such as newspapers, investing, advertising on corporate giving, jewelry shopping, bathroom remodeling. A wide age range works well if respondents share an interest or when age is irrelevant.

Myth 5

It is a mistake to ask respondents "why" they do or feel something. Often, they are unaware of their real motivations, and the question itself can be threatening.

REALITY: Usually it's not the question that is the problem; it's the way the question is asked. "Why?" can be asked in an intimidating way. Asked gently, however, the question shows genuine interest and a desire to understand, which respondents may find flattering. Good researchers do not rely solely on direct "why" questions to understand underlying motives. These are analyzed together with respondents' other attitudes and behaviors.

Myth 6

Qualitative research should rely mainly on projective techniques, such as collages, drawings, photographs, brand "obituaries," and role-playing. These bring out thoughts and feelings that consumers either are not in touch with or are uncomfortable acknowledging publicly.

REALITY: Projective methods are excellent tools, but they should not take the place of direct questions. In many areas, straightforward nonjudgmental questions about respondents' feelings successfully uncover emotions.

Projective tools help free respondents to express their

feelings. They are especially useful in commodity categories, for which respondents tend to say that all the brands are alike; in low-involvement categories, such as detergents and deodorants, which consumers feel embarrassed to admit are important to them; and with teenagers, who usually are hesitant to express themselves. Certain projective questions also are comfortable for most respondents, such as asking them what a brand's image is or how they picture a product's users.

However, there are some drawbacks of projective techniques. Respondents, especially executives, can become irritated when they are unable to voice their views directly but must, instead, play what they consider childish games.

Techniques like collages are quite time-consuming. If direct questions seem to be producing honest emotional responses, it may be equally effective and more time-efficient to go that route.

Asking direct questions from a number of different angles often is effective. Moderators need to talk in terms of respondents' "feelings," not "opinions" or what they consider "important," questions that illicit more rational reactions.

Myth 7

Focus groups at 8 p.m. are not a good idea because everyone is tired.

REALITY: Focus groups at 6 p.m. and 8 p.m. are necessary because most people have jobs or are involved in a business.

Usually, the energy level of a focus group is more indicative of the chemistry of the respondents and their interest in the topic than the time. Most 8 p.m. focus groups are fine. In fact, some of the best groups we've conducted have been at this time.

Myth 8

The sign of a good moderator is that he or she says very little in a focus group.

REALITY: In the ideal focus group, respondents speak one at a time, stick to the subject, offer detailed explanations of their answers without going on too long, and give constructive criticism of the client's ideas. But the ideal focus group doesn't occur often. If respondents were so well-behaved, moderators might not be needed. We see the moderator's role as active — both responsive and creative.

That role includes guiding the group dynamics. In addition, moderators should offer non-leading feedback by reflecting back to respondents what the moderator picks up to probe further. For example, a moderator can ask, "What I seem to be hearing is. . . . Is that true?"

An experienced moderator can sense when respondents are open, following up with questions to reach a deeper level. Also, moderators should follow up on hypotheses developed before the research or from earlier focus groups if these issues do not arise unaided.

A good moderator does not simply ask the questions in the topic guide but follows up on interesting or new ideas relevant to the research issues. And moderators should look for solutions to the client's problems. If respondents reject the product or concept statement, the moderator should first ask for suggestions in an open-ended manner, then probe reactions to possible ideas that come to mind.

Active moderating is not the same as asking leading questions. When probing questions are asked in a neutral manner, respondents feel free to say what they believe and will give more information.

Myth 9

Recruiting is fairly easy when the client provides lists of customers to be interviewed for focus groups and depth interviews.

REALITY: There's no question that without such lists it would be difficult, if not impossible, to recruit specific types of low-incidence people — recent purchasers of a luxury product or subscribers to a small-circulation publication, for example. But recruiting from a list is not necessarily easy. Even when using lists, recruiting questions are still needed. For example, a list may have a magazine subscription in a man's name when a woman is the real reader.

Myth 10

Sending notes to the moderator during the focus group enables clients to be involved in the process, ensuring that the research provides answers to their questions.

REALITY: Repeated notes brought into the interviewing room can be quite disruptive. Clients need and deserve to be part of the process, but unless the client is convinced the moderator is going in the wrong direction or providing incorrect information, it's best to resist the temptation.

Myth 11

Focus groups should be used rarely since there is almost always a strong personality who dominates the discussion.

REALITY: In many groups, respondents all contribute to the discussion, even though, of course, some people are more talkative or articulate than others. A strong personality may speak up confidently, even loudly, yet not dominate. Instead, other respondents may distance themselves from that person, feeling free to disagree. It's not unusual for a respondent to say that others' comments triggered a memory that an interviewer's questions alone might not have brought to mind.

Experienced moderators have a variety of techniques for dealing with respondents who have strong personalities. For example, having respondents write down their reactions to materials or about a brand is a good way of having them "commit" prior to group discussions. It provides a reality check for clients and researchers, too. We can look at what respondents wrote rather than debating whether someone led the discussion.

Myth 12

The topic guide and materials shown in a series of focus groups should be kept the same throughout for consistency.

REALITY: The beauty of qualitative research is that it is dynamic. Some question areas turn out to be rich, others draw little response. New ideas may come up, which should alter the topic guide during the study. Changes usually mean that learning has taken place.

Modifications also can be made in materials such as concept statements for a new product. They can be rewritten to eliminate negative words and phrases to clarify areas of confusion, or to add new benefits. It's best to do this after obtaining responses in at least two sessions. The purpose of the qualitative study is to help the client move toward ideas that work, not to "quantify" that an idea doesn't work.

Myth 13

Qualitative research studies should always be followed by quantitative research to test the hypotheses.

REALITY: Aside from budget constraints, there are solid research reasons why and situations in which a qualitative study may be sufficient:

- If the results of a sizable qualitative study are very consistent and have "common sense validity."

- If the purpose of the qualitative research is to develop ideas that will then be explored further. An example might be finding out what consumer needs are in order to create new product concepts, which will be shown in subsequent qualitative research.

- If there is little or no expense in trying out the ideas coming out of the qualitative research—and little or no risk.

- If the purpose of the research is to identify "red flags"— words or ideas that strike an immediate negative chord.

Myth 14

A discussion guide for focus groups is referred to by some clients as "a script," a term that implies that the moderator should follow it pretty much verbatim.

REALITY: A topic guide should be just that—a general guide of the topics that should be covered, the order in which they should be covered, and some ideas on possible probes or techniques the moderator might use.

Certain aspects of the guide should be kept in sequence, while others are not as important. For instance, general questions usually are best asked before specific ones. The sequence is merely a guideline, though, when there is no significant research reason for holding off on a subject until another one has been discussed.

Each focus group has its own rhythm, and the moderator should try to harness its energy. If respondents become animated about a subject, an effective moderator follows up right away. To cut respondents off and move on to another question can dissipate energy that the group may not regain. The "seize-the-moment" style of moderating feels more spontaneous and conversational to respondents, and because it seems natural and unforced, they are more likely to open up.

Clients should not expect questions to be asked in the exact order they appear in the topic guide. Some may not even be asked the same way they are phrased in the topic guide.

Myth 15

Qualitative research and in-depth interviews must be

done in person, rather than over the telephone to develop rapport between interviewer and respondent.

REALITY: Rapport can be just as strong or stronger in telephone interviews. Not being able to see the interviewer can be an advantage. For instance, because respondents can only guess at the interviewer's age, they are less likely to worry about offending the interviewer with comments like, "That's for old people." To build rapport on the phone, we ease into the interview with simple usage or attitude questions such as, "How often do you read the newspaper?" rather than the icebreakers often asked in focus groups, e.g., "What comes to mind when you think of [the product category]?" Usually, after a short time, respondents are just as comfortable and open in a telephone interview as they would be in an in-person interview.

INDEX